BUSINESS UPGRADE

BUSINESS UPGRADE

21 days to reignite the
entrepreneurial spirit in
you and your team

RICHARD PARKES CORDOCK

CAPSTONE

First published 2007 by
Capstone Publishing Limited (a Wiley Company)
The Atrium
Southern Gate
Chichester
West Sussex
PO19 8SQ
www.wileyeurope.com
Email (for orders and customer service enquires): cs-books@wiley.co.uk

CIP catalogue records for this book are available from the British Library and the US Library of Congress

ISBN 13:   978-1-84112-744-6
ISBN 10:   1-84112-744-2

Typeset in Swiss 11/16pt by Sparks, Oxford (www.sparks.co.uk)
Printed and bound in Great Britain by TJ International Ltd, Padstow, Cornwall

This book is printed on acid-free paper responsibly manufactured from sustainable forestry in which at least two trees are planted for each one used for paper production.

Substantial discounts on bulk quantities of Capstone Books are available to corporations, professional associations and other organizations.
For details telephone John Wiley & Sons on (+44) 1243-770441, fax (+44) 1243 770571 or email corporatedevelopment@wiley.co.uk

For my brother Mark –
a shining example of how to achieve results
against all odds

CONTENTS

ACKNOWLEDGEMENTS

As with any creative project, it is a team effort that turns thoughts into reality. This has certainly been the case with the creation of *Business Upgrade* and along the way there are many people I must thank for their contribution and help.

Firstly, I must thank Anna Rushton, who is my true creative catalyst. It is only through Anna's coaching and guidance that this book can be the reality it is. In the same breath, I must thank Nuala Mullen who edited this book. Nuala's editing brings a sharpness and flow, which has made it the joy I hope you find it to read.

Books cannot be written without inspiration and for that I must thank all the business leaders and entrepreneurs I have interviewed over the past few years. It is their words that I have interpreted for this book. There are also those I have not met but who have had a direct impact on me. These include Sam Walton for his total customer dedication, Lou Gerstner and Jack Welsh for their entrepreneurial leadership and J.W. Marriot for making me truly understand the power of people.

Closer to home I would like to thank B.J. Cunningham, Simon Woodroffe and Llew Harris for unknowingly influencing my thoughts.

This book is drawn from my experiences in my corporate days. I would therefore like to acknowledge and thank my numerous colleagues who I shared many happy experiences with.

Lastly, I must thank my family and friends who helped and encouraged me in writing this book. Special thanks to my parents (whose house we borrowed when I wrote this book) and my wife and daughter for their love and never ending support.

PREFACE

Business Upgrade is the natural follow-on from my first book, *Millionaire Upgrade*. Interestingly enough, it takes me back in time to my previous career when I worked for a large international software company. I spent many happy and relatively successful years working in that world, until one day when I was fired! It was not the last time in my career that I was fired; in fact, after completing my MBA (Masters of Business Administration) and taking another job in the software industry, it happened again! That's when I realized that the corporate world was not for me and that my future lay in becoming an entrepreneur. It turned out to be the best thing that could have happened to me.

It is only since starting my own business and studying in depth the inner thinking of successful entrepreneurs and their leadership styles and, most importantly, having had the benefit of selling products and services to my own customers, that I have been able to look again at my corporate days and realize what was missing – and what I believe many other people are missing too.

It was not long after completing my MBA that I researched and developed Millionaire MBA™ Business Mentoring Programme. I wanted to pass on the knowledge I had gained from real-life entrepreneurs, which is not taught at business school. It is from that base, and from my own previous experience in the corporate world, that *Business Upgrade* was written.

The story that follows – of Lucy being assigned to a special project within a large corporation – actually happened to me. I spent over eight years working for the same software company until I became disillusioned and lost belief, but not before taking on a special project at HQ after our company had gone through a major merger and acquisition. During my years there, working predominantly in business consulting, I always felt I had two careers. The first took me into many different companies around the world where I met numerous people at all levels and saw how different companies were run and managed. My second 'career' involved studying in depth at a micro and macro level the company I had worked for over so many years. I had joined the company not long after it had been floated on the stock market, at a time when it was awash with cash. Like many newly-floated companies, it was ambitious in its growth plans but ultimately it struggled and stalled. This was chiefly because the entrepreneurial drive that had taken the company from a standing start to a large international organization was lost as wave after wave of new employees focused more on the share price value than on the customer. Millions of that newly acquired capital was wasted on prestigious corporate offices, large executive salary packages and luxury business travel, rather than investing in innovation, product development and building customer trust.

As a result of starting my own company and the research I have undertaken, I have been fortunate to meet many entrepreneurs and gain a clear understanding from them of what makes their companies so successful. Without a doubt, there is a 180 degree shift from the thinking of smaller entrepreneurial businesses to that of larger corporations. Some companies are able to continue growing from their entrepreneurial roots: Richard Branson's Virgin group is an obvious example of a company that has managed this. Interestingly enough, so has General Electric, which was originally formed over 100 years ago by Thomas Edison, the inventor of the electric light bulb. GE is now one of the the largest companies in the world and still true to its entrepreneurial roots. It is no surprise that the principles set out in this book are consistent in all successful, innovative companies that see themselves as entrepreneurial thinkers rather than corporate bureaucracies.

Larger companies are often scared of the word 'entrepreneur', thinking that if employees are entrepreneurial thinkers they will run off and start their own businesses. In reality, all companies must be entrepreneurial in their thinking, because it was their very entrepreneurial thinking that made them great in the first place. It is only entrepreneurial thinking that can drive the change and innovation that will allow the business to compete in an ever-changing and more competitive global economy.

Companies that fail to see themselves as entrepreneurial will fail to keep pace with the constantly changing needs of their customers and ultimately will be overtaken by smaller, more nimble organizations who can meet the needs of customers. No large company is immune to this. Whenever you read this book, there will be examples in the newspapers of large corporate companies, who have stood the test of time for years, being threatened by smaller start-ups or other large organizations who are more entrepreneurial in their thinking and who welcome change and innovation.

It is often said that change, death and taxes are the only constants in life. Companies therefore need to embrace change and not resist it. They need to understand the changing needs of their customers and listen to them, rather than dictate to them what they will buy. They need to understand the changing world and embrace the opportunity that this brings. Who better for large companies to learn from than the masters of change, innovation and opportunity – entrepreneurs!

Richard Parkes Cordock, June 2006

INTRODUCTION

Business Upgrade extends the thinking and concept of I BELIEVE, first introduced in *Millionaire Upgrade* and adds a further two principles of WE BELIEVE and THEY BELIEVE.

For a fuller insight into enterprise leadership and the philosophy of I BELIEVE, you will benefit from reading *Millionaire Upgrade*. Although these principles were written with the self-employed entrepreneur in mind, the ideas and thinking apply equally to larger organizations. When reading *Millionaire Upgrade*, please make the mental substitution of the word 'entrepreneur' with the word 'enterprise leader' – as it is enterprise leadership and thinking that is required in the corporate world. In many ways, the role of an enterprise leader within a larger organization is more challenging than that of an entrepreneur operating in the outside world – simply because the internal enterprise leader has more stubborn obstacles and challenges to overcome, namely co-workers, management and the company's resistance to change. Enterprise Leadership is about adopting a mindset focused on a common and collective goal, embracing change and innovation for a common purpose. Every one of us has the ability to inspire that change and innovation in our organization. Each of us can adopt the mindset of the enterprise leader. In doing so we are directly contributing to the company's inevitable success.

Whilst reading this book, I ask you to live and breathe these three key concepts:

- **I BELIEVE** – you, the leader
- **WE BELIEVE** – the team
- **THEY BELIEVE** – the customer

Business is all about belief and without the alignment of belief with the customer, the employees and the leadership of the company at all levels, from top to bottom, then success and growth will prove elusive. Every aspect of our lives, professional and personal, is built on belief and it is clear that by extension so too is your business!

DISCLAIMER

Amroze Technology, the organization featured in this book, is a purely fictional company and is the accumulation of my experience of the hundreds of companies I visited in my consulting career. In fact, Amroze is named after my daughter Amelia Rose and exists only within these pages. All the characters are fictitious and named mostly after friends and family. Any resemblance to any other company or person is purely coincidental and wholly unintentional.

PROLOGUE

It was Monday morning and Lucy was adding the finishing touches to the training pack she was putting together. The truth was she didn't really have enough to occupy her and that was a new experience for her. After four challenging years working in Amroze Technology's overseas offices she had been delighted to be recalled to Head Office, the nerve centre of the company, but for the past month she had been doing what she privately thought of as 'time-filler work'. It had been clear to her from day one of her return that no one really had a job for her yet so she had been given the task of developing a training programme for new graduate entrants. She had accepted the task with good grace, even though it hadn't taken her long to realise that Amroze hadn't recruited any new graduates in the last year and it didn't look likely that any would be coming along soon either, given the current problems in the company. It was just one of a number of signs she had seen that things were not going well, and in part she attributed that to the fact that between her recall and her arrival, the company had suffered a major blow. The CEO of just 18 months had suffered a second heart attack within a year, and although not immediately life threatening, he had taken it for the warning that it clearly was and had resigned due to ill health. The gossip in the company was that it was the huge stress and pressure he was under due to Amroze's problems in the market place that had brought on the second attack. The rumour mill had plenty to work with: the CEO had been faced with some serious problems over the last year. He, like a number of his predecessors over the last five years, had failed to turn the fortunes of the ailing company around. It was obvious to everyone that sales had taken a serious nose dive and their customers were leaving them at an increasing rate.

Lucy was only too aware what this kind of pressure had done to the CEO's health. He had only managed a brief meeting with her on her arrival and within a couple of weeks he had stepped down due to ill health and left immediately. The board had been looking to appoint a successor ever since and it needed to be soon as the feeling in the building was one of stagnation; everyone was just waiting for something to happen. Lucy glanced at her calendar to check a meeting time for later that day and saw she had written 'new CEO appointed?' against today's date. According to Claire in reception there would be an announcement later today. Claire's information, as always well researched, was based on the fact that her friend Amy in the press office had been put on alert to put out an announcement to the media and internally throughout the company and to keep Monday morning clear for that. 'Well I hope it's somebody who is willing to shake the place up a bit and give me something real to do,' thought Lucy as she turned back again to the document that needed only a final checking before she would hand it over.

At that moment Claire was eyeing the middle-aged man who was waiting by her reception desk for the chairman's PA to come and collect him. Claire prided herself for being naturally in the front line for company gossip and as soon as he had announced himself as 'Stephen Fox to see the chairman' she had been gathering impressions to circulate through the grapevine. Any observations were cut short as the lift doors opened and she saw it was the chairman himself, not his PA, who came to greet him. Now that was interesting, so it looked like the rumours were true. Claire had greeted all of the board members on their arrival that morning and she knew there were no absentees as there often were. She clearly heard the chairman saying 'Stephen we are delighted you have agreed to join us and I know the board is really looking forward to meeting you' as the lift doors closed on the two men. Claire thought: 'New CEO? Now that's interesting.' A little over an hour later she saw Stephen Fox coming out of the lift, looking very pleased with himself. He stopped by her desk and politely asked her if she could contact Lucy Robinson for him. Claire directed him to a visitor phone where she had Lucy waiting on the line and she heard him asking if Lucy was free for an early lunch. He obviously got the answer he wanted because he smiled and ended the call by saying he would wait in reception. He waved his thanks to Claire and then wandered over to the seating area and began making phone calls, which, try as she might, Claire couldn't quite hear.

Chapter One

Lucy put the phone down and sat staring at it for a moment. She was delighted to have heard from Stephen as they had been good friends when they had done their MBA together and any excuse to get out of the office was welcome. More importantly, she didn't think it was a social visit. Putting two and two together she had a pretty good idea that he was the new CEO. There was no other reason for him to be at Amroze Technology on a Monday morning and he had sounded quite fired up. 'Great, I'm going to be the first to get the inside story,' she thought as she logged off and headed downstairs.

Stephen hadn't changed that much, a little older maybe but he still had that good humoured, intelligent manner. She was delighted to see him again and as they settled at a table in the small Italian restaurant around the corner from the office she could see that he was a man big with news. She hadn't missed Claire's speculative glance as they had walked out of reception either and had seen her mouthing 'New CEO!' to her as they passed her desk. As it happened, Stephen himself was happy to confirm it and told her the announcement was being made that day and he would be joining in just three weeks' time.

'Of course I was delighted when you e-mailed me a couple of months ago saying you were coming back to Amroze's Head Office. I was looking forward to catching up with you, but I certainly didn't think we'd be working together!'

Lucy was sincere in her delight. 'Congratulations, Stephen, you deserve it and I am really pleased for you, and of course for us!' Their friendship from their MBA days had been unexpected, given the age difference and the experience gap between them, but it was based on a genuine mutual respect for each other and they had kept in touch over the years. Back then, Lucy was just starting out, and Stephen was already a well established businessman who was taking time out to consolidate his career, but for the period of their studies at least, they were equals. In fact, it turned out they shared a similar outlook and attitude to business that had united them in their studies. What Stephen then started to explain made her sit up straight and wonder if she was really hearing him right.

'Lucy, I've taken this job because I know Amroze Technology needs turning round and I believe I can do that. But, I can't do it without help and what I need is the real truth about the state the company is in. Because I know how you work, and the kind of person you are, I know I can trust you to deliver an honest report, giving me the information I need before I start officially in three weeks. From what I remember of your career at Amroze, you've pretty much experienced all areas of the company, both at head office and overseas and now you're back this could be the perfect project for you. Also, I gather from the speed with which you came to lunch you don't have anything very pressing on at the moment do you?' He was laughing at this point and Lucy joined in. He knew her too well to think she would drop an important piece of work to go to lunch with an old friend and she confirmed that yes, she was between projects and would love a new challenge.

'Well, I can promise you that. What I want is for you to go into the various departments of the company, get feedback on what people are really thinking about Amroze, what works, and what doesn't work for them right now. I want honest opinions, not what they think I want to hear, so you will have to push and probe a bit. Talk to everyone, heads of departments, VPs and employees in each of the line roles, so I get a complete picture before I come in. So Lucy, what do you think? Will you take it on?'

Lucy felt a surge of excitement at this request. This was more like it! She felt pleased Stephen had so much faith in her, and energized at the prospect of a real job to get her teeth into. But also, if she was honest, it was a bit daunting as well. One thought immediately sprung to mind and she knew she had to raise it with Stephen.

'I'd love to do it, but I have one concern. I've been working at the overseas offices for four years now and while I have a good idea of what the potential problems with the company are, I am a bit out of touch with head office. I'm not sure how the VPs and department heads will take me coming in and grilling them.'

Stephen nodded. 'Yes, I have thought of that, but in fact your being new to them is an advantage as you come at it without prejudice. I have also asked the chairman to include a paragraph in the announcement of my appointment to the staff. I suggested he says that I have given you a special project to undertake and that you will be reporting directly to me. I am asking everyone to give you full cooperation and be totally upfront and honest with you so that I can start making Amroze Technology an effective company that will benefit everyone. If you encounter any problems refer them directly to me, and that should give you a clear entry. At least I hope so.'

Lucy thought about it, and appreciated that he had given her a virtual 'letter of credit' so that she could go anywhere and ask anything. This was definitely an assignment to keep her occupied. 'Stephen, I really appreciate this.'

'Well, tell me that again when you have finished! I've already secured a structure that will give you some support. You will be getting your own office and secretary as I want to keep this material entirely confidential until I am ready to share it. Of course it won't be a very big office, but at least the chairman has promised you something.'

'If it's a broom cupboard it will be an improvement on what I have now. You were only appointed a few hours ago; this is moving very fast, isn't it?'

Stephen shrugged, 'Not really, I've been planning since I was first approached about the job. To be honest, I didn't want to wait until it was confirmed by the board because I would have lost valuable time. I know what I need, and that's to see right down to the blood and the bone of the organization and you can find that out for me. Lucy, I want you to understand that from what I have seen, Amroze is in serious trouble. I am telling you this in confidence so you can see why I need to get things moving as fast as possible to try to turn the situation around.

'You have just three weeks to get me the information I need. I believe I only have a year at most before Amroze has to call it a day. If things are allowed to continue as they are then none of us will have a job. I don't want to scare you, but those are the facts. I took this job on because of the challenge and because I've turned round companies in as bad a situation as Amroze before, and I believe it can be done here. The board believe that and that's why they are giving me everything I've asked for, and that includes getting you on this project.

'I appreciate you may need some outside help so I am also asking a guy called Tom McMillan to mentor you through these next few weeks. I brought him into my last company to help with some of the managers and he has lots of great ideas that I believe we will benefit from. Also, I think you will enjoy working with him. Like you, he doesn't suffer fools gladly!'

Now this was really looking like a serious project. Lucy was already starting to think about how she would tackle the task, in fact she was itching to get started, but Stephen still had more to tell her about her new mentor.

'Tom taught me a great business philosophy that I know is what we need to put in place at Amroze. It's all about the three levels of belief, the combination of which makes the difference between a successful and a non-successful business. Tom will tell you all about it himself, probably better than I can!'

'Sounds good to me, how do I get in touch with him?'

'Well, I've rung his PA and she has set up a meeting for you at the Convention Centre at the airport at 11.30am tomorrow. You must have lots of other questions but we'd better give that waiter our order or he'll have us thrown out for loitering!' They both turned their attention to the menu and spent the rest of lunch catching up and discussing some key things to look out for over the coming weeks. Later, on her return to the office she found a mail saying that her new office would be ready the following morning. She just had to box up her things that evening and they would be moved for her. Lucy couldn't keep the smile off her face and her colleagues were giving her inquiring looks. The news of her lunch with the new CEO had obviously spread, because also in her inbox was the promised memo from the chairman to all the staff in which she was named. She took a deep breath – the game was on.

Chapter Two

Before leaving for the day, Lucy wanted to make a start at least on organizing her thoughts on her new project. If she only had three weeks to deliver, every minute was going to count. Even in the few weeks she had been back, it had been obvious to her that the company was currently performing under par and putting it right was going to be a huge task. However, Stephen had been confident he could turn the company round; what he wanted from her was the information to do it with. 'OK, let's make a start,' she thought as she opened up her laptop and began typing up some initial thoughts. As she typed, it was soon clear that she had given more thought to Amroze's situation than she realized.

Thinking about it, Lucy knew that the problems had been growing since Amroze was listed on the stock market. Although a lot of capital had been raised, most of it had been squandered trying, without much success, to break into new markets. Charlie Gardham, the entrepreneur who started Amroze, had left the company not long after it went public and that was the point at which things started to change. A new team of professional managers were brought in and they could not have been more different from Charlie with his passionate enthusiasm and commitment. Amroze had replaced the CEO a number of times in a half-hearted attempt to address the challenges that the transition to public listed company had thrown up but none of them ever seemed to be able to find out what was really going wrong. She stopped typing at that point as the realization had surprised her. Lucy, like everyone else, had thought that going public was a good thing at the time. Now it was clear that it had changed the company almost beyond recognition; no more passion and enthusiasm. Instead it was all about meeting the market's expectation and quarter-to-quarter results.

Over lunch, Stephen had made it clear that what he had seen when he looked at the company was not good. Their customers were leaving to go to their competitors, and sales revenue was down. Their lack of focus and direction was apparent in the market place and, even worse, they were sending out a confused message that customers could not understand. Lucy herself knew that the current range of products was poor and had no clear competitive advantage and she had watched as the recent mass exodus of staff became public knowledge in the industry, making their position even shakier.

After listening to his summary, Lucy had asked Stephen why he wanted to take on the challenge of new CEO when things looked so bad. His reply had only partly reassured her. He reminded her that his reputation was as someone who was astute and who never got involved in companies that he didn't believe were fundamentally sound, whatever they looked like to the market. She had ended up agreeing with him that getting a full detailed analysis of the company before he started was a good idea – now it was up to her to deliver it and that was the part that unnerved her a little. She had three weeks to get to the bottom of why the company had been floundering in recent years. One thing was for sure, she had a lot to get to grips with.

Leaning back in her chair she ran through her thinking so far, trying to establish a starting point for her project. Her earlier thoughts about when she had first worked at the company returned to the time when Charlie Gardham was still there. It was, she realized, a totally different place then, fun and exciting with every day bringing a challenge to be met with pleasure and creativity. Shaking her head and smiling at the memory she wondered just where that buzz and energy had gone.

A sudden understanding made her sit up and start typing again. If there was one problem with the company, it was that it had lost its spark and its direction. Thinking about Charlie had made her realize what was missing, and it wasn't just that Charlie was no longer there. Something had happened to make people stop caring about the company and that was when things had started to change.

Saving the file, she knew she needed more information on the man Stephen had chosen to mentor her so she could get an idea of how he might approach the project with her. She ran a search on 'Tom McMillan'. His name had quite a few hits. She clicked on his webpage and began to read, keen to find out why Stephen had particularly wanted him. On the site was a description of the work he had done with companies like theirs, and as she flicked through the links she kept piecing it together with parts of Stephen's conversation. She could see that Tom's track record in this area was excellent and then suddenly a phrase leaped out at her: 'reigniting the entrepreneurial spirit within companies'. With a rush of recognition she realized that this was what Charlie had been interested in, and that this was what all her memories of Amroze had been about. That was what was missing. They needed to recapture the essence of when Charlie started the company and experience again that rush of enthusiasm, energy and creativity.

Lucy next clicked on a link where she could read an extract from a book Tom had written. The more preparation she did on Tom, the more confident she would feel when she met him.

Chapter 2a

Lucy arrived at the Convention Centre a little early for her meeting with Tom McMillan. She settled herself into one of the large sofas in a corner of the lobby. While she waited she took out of her briefcase the printout she had downloaded from Tom's website the day before. She reread her notes, wanting to make a good impression on him, partly, as she admitted to herself, because of Stephen's good opinion of him, but she was also sure he would be reporting her progress back to Stephen, though that hadn't been actually been mentioned. Having a mentor was not something new to Lucy; she had been on the graduate fast track and had automatically been assigned mentors during many of her major moves in the company, but this was the first time she had been offered an external mentor and she wasn't quite sure if the process would be the same. Skimming through the material, Lucy headlined the areas she could see were most relevant and it was apparent that Tom was in great demand as a speaker at business events and conferences as well as to companies worldwide. Cynically, Lucy had thought this might be just to promote his book, but on closer inspection she could see that the theme running through all her material was Tom's real passion for working with companies to effect change. He talked a lot about reigniting the entrepreneurial spirit in companies and Lucy had underlined that phrase several times as it had made such an impression on her when she had seen it on his website.

She heard a burst of applause from behind the double doors on the other side of the lobby and after a moment, two people walked out together. One clearly was Tom, she recognized him from his photo on his website, and the other was a much older man who looked familiar but she could not place him. As the men parted company with a handshake, Tom spotted her and walked briskly over. He extended his hand and with a warm smile said, 'You must be Lucy; I'm Tom McMillan. Very pleased to meet you.' He settled himself into the comfortable club chair opposite to her and waved away her thanks with a smile as she told him how grateful she was that he was able to meet her at such short notice.

'No problem, and it's Stephen you should thank,' said Tom. 'He told me it was urgent and as he and I have worked together before I was delighted to help out.' Lucy was still puzzling over who Tom had left the conference with and as it worked as a good ice breaker, she asked Tom who he was.

'That's Michael Redford; his picture is often in the business magazines.' He looked to see if she recognized the name and she gave a slight shake of her head. 'He's very well known in his field, and certainly very highly regarded as a successful entrepreneur. There's an interesting story behind how I met him; we spent a long plane journey together and what I learned from just talking to him encouraged me to make significant changes in my life. He had a philosophy about business success, based on belief, and you could say he was the catalyst that took my business life in a whole new direction. In fact, his three-fold system of belief is probably why Stephen asked me to mentor you on this project as he has successfully implemented it himself in his previous companies.'

This was the second time this 'theory' about belief had come up and Lucy wanted to hear more, but first Tom asked her to tell him a little about the meeting she had had with Stephen the day before. He knew that Stephen would take over in three weeks and she explained to Tom that her challenge was to complete a special project for him, which meant she had to provide a full analysis and recommendation of what she thought of the company and its future prospects.

Tom listened to her with great attention, occasionally nodding at a point she made and then asked her to give him more details on how she viewed Amroze.

Lucy outlined the major issues from her preliminary research: the drop-off in sales and fall in share price, loss of market share, lack of direction for the company and overall low staff morale. Tom's attention was so complete and sympathetic that she found herself telling him about Charlie and what the company had been like when he ran it.

'I don't think I am just being fanciful and seeing that time through rose-tinted glasses. I really feel that things were different when he was around and before the company was floated on the stock exchange.'

This was just as Tom had suspected and he began to speak.

'What you have just explained to me is a classic situation that happens to just about every growing company that reaches a certain size. Believe me, I have seen this so many times in companies worldwide.'

Lucy was not sure that reassured her, and he must have seen a look of concern on her face.

'Don't worry, it is a pattern that is very predicable, and thankfully very fixable.' At this point, Tom paused and reached into his pocket to bring out a brown leather-covered notebook which he slid across the coffee table to Lucy. 'This is one of the first things I learned from my mentor – always carry a notebook.' Lucy had been about to open her diary to write down his comments but she reached forward and took it from him. She looked enquiringly at Tom and he smiled back at her. 'It's yours, I give one to each person I mentor so you have a permanent record, in one place, of all the things we discuss. You will find it invaluable to be able to refer back to, and to add your own comments as they occur to you.'

Lucy thanked him and turned to the first page as she got ready to make some notes.

'You can pick any company, any big multinational, and they will all have experienced the same problem. I suspect even large multinational companies such as IBM, Apple and the Ford Motor company will not have escaped this pattern at some point.' Lucy looked a bit uncertain, so he went on. 'Go back 100 years to when Ford was created. I'm sure that Henry Ford would have experienced the very same issues when his company reached a certain size that I believe you are experiencing now.'

'Well it's certainly good news to know that we're not alone!' was Lucy's comment.

'Certainly not,' came back Tom, 'and the good news is that your problems can be fixed, but it will require your company to take extensive action and that's why Stephen is so keen to have you do this report. You don't take action without having all the information to make decisions with.' Sensing Lucy's eagerness he went on. 'You of course want to know how we do this, what the solution is; is that right?' She nodded, smiling and he continued. 'I mentioned belief before, and that is the foundation of what needs to change at Amroze. To do that you need to talk to as many people as you can at all levels in the company and once you have established what exactly is going wrong in each of these areas, then you will be able to start to effect real change.

'I think you already have an inkling of what needs to change, because the way you talk about Charlie and the company's early days shows me that you can identify what is missing. I believe Amroze needs to get back to its original entrepreneurial roots and find the essence of what made the company great in the first place. As I said before, all companies experience these problems when they move from being an entrepreneurial start-up to a mature and stable company. Sooner or later the problems you are currently experiencing will occur, it is inevitable.'

Lucy interrupted him, 'Are you saying we couldn't have avoided it?' Tom shook his head.

'No, not quite that. Let me explain a bit further and that should give you some clues for what you need to do to fix the situation. You hit the nail on the head when you spoke of times being different when Charlie, the original founder, was there. He clearly knew how to get results and I suspect he was someone who succeeded even when everything was against him, against all odds if you like.'

Lucy nodded in agreement. 'Yep, he thrived on challenge; everything was a real buzz to him.'

'Most companies are typically started by an entrepreneur; someone who is full of passion, belief, drive and determination, and is focused on a vision that they really want to bring into being. It is the pure energy of the entrepreneur that is able to drive the company forward. Now, up to a certain size, the entrepreneur can still have a direct impact on the business and that vision, direction and passion of the entrepreneur, coupled with the belief he or she is able to instil in the team, can make the company achieve miracles in the face of total adversity. It's pretty much the same story in most companies. Think back to the beginnings of Microsoft. Wasn't that the vision of Bill Gates, and his total belief in what a computer could, and should, do?'

Lucy was certainly familiar with the Microsoft story as it formed the cornerstone of many a lecture on their business MBA course but she had thought their success was down to the brilliance of the product, not the personality of the founder or his partner, Paul Allen. She voiced this to Tom, and was surprised by his answer.

'Of course the product has to be right, but it is the leadership of the entrepreneur and their belief in themselves, their product and their team that makes it happen. If you combine that with a team which also has that level of belief, and an ability to make customers believe in the company too, then that virtually guarantees that you will put that new start-up business on the map.' Relaxing a little he leaned back and Lucy did the same. 'You said you joined Amroze Technology just a few years after it started. What was it like then?'

'Well, Charlie Gardham, the founder, was still there and he was certainly an individual character. You're right; he always had a clear and persuasive vision of what we were creating and really had a way of keeping us driving forward. He never took the customers for granted and would do absolutely anything to make them happy. I remember he had this "motto",' she was laughing as she remembered it, 'he would have us repeating "Customers and Cash" just like a mantra as if our lives depended on it. We thought it was amusing at first, but it really focused us on what he was about. For Charlie the customer was king so we spent our time getting new customers, and then keeping them by really looking after them and their interests.'

Tom was intrigued and remarked that Charlie sounded like his sort of businessman. 'Yes, I think you would have liked him. He kept on at us that we must never run out of cash for the business and that cash came from the pockets of our customers and our job was to make sure that they were happy and continued giving us their cash, because for Charlie everything was about cash flow.' She was struck by a thought and her expression became a little reflective. 'We don't really talk like that anymore. Now we speak about share price and what's happening to it. I'd say for most people in the company, the last thing they think about is customers and cash.' She realised she was sounding a little sad, and from the expression on Tom's face he had realized how she was feeling. He didn't say anything, so she carried on with her train of thought.

'You know, Tom, I really believed Charlie loved the customers and I believe they loved him back! There was certainly a kind of fan club between him and his customers and vice versa. He wasn't remote; they knew they could always ring him with problems, or even suggestions for improvements. He loved to hear from them and he couldn't do enough for them, which they really appreciated. You would hear time and time again from customers about how much they valued the service they got from Charlie, and also I guess the personal interest he showed in them and their problems.'

Although he was fairly sure he already knew the answer, Tom still asked the question anyway.

'What do think changed?'

Lucy didn't want to just jump straight in, but she took a moment to consider her answer, based on what she had just said and what she had heard from Tom. 'I think what changed is that we became a bigger company and once we had floated on the stock market Charlie took his money and left. I really think it has never quite been the same since.'

That was pretty much what Tom had expected to hear and he now needed some more information from her. 'What size of company are you now?' This was easy, as statistics were Lucy's life blood and she had been jotting down various figures over the last couple of days. 'We have over 2000 staff and 14 offices around the world. We have over 20,000 clients currently; I guess you would call us a sizeable company.'

Tom again nodded in agreement. 'You certainly are sizeable and what you have just described is a typical growth challenge. Businesses, like economics and politics, are predictably cyclical, you know. What you are going through now is no different from the pattern that many other companies have experienced. The typical picture looks something like this, and I bet you it is the same for Amroze Technology. Here's how it usually goes. An energetic passionate entrepreneur has an idea for a business that will fix a problem for a customer. He probably has very few resources, in either cash or assets – but he definitely has a compelling vision that he is able to communicate. Because of his passion and belief, people start to believe in him too. He is able to raise money, get a small team together and they all work hard towards a common purpose. There will be many problems along the way, but his resolve is so strong that he can break through anything with pure tenacity and persistence.

'As a new company they have no cash or customers, so they have to focus on both of these key elements. Charlie was absolutely right when he had you using those words "cash and customers". The rest of the team are so close to the new business that they too totally understand how important cash and customers are. Without customers, there is no cash; without cash, nobody will get paid at the end of the month! The team gets so involved in the company that they absorb the passion, belief and energy of the entrepreneur and now you have a team of passionately believing employees, effectively a "dream team" that can achieve anything it sets its mind to. Each of these employees is an "enterprise leader" and I want you to keep this title in mind because we'll delve into it much later on.'

Lucy was listening intently, and her pen was literally flying over the pages, but what Tom was saying brought back an image sharply into her mind. It was of the early days of working with Charlie and of the many late nights with all the team in his office, boxes of pizza on the table and the arguments, discussions and energy as they batted ideas around, and brainstormed ways to improve or develop their products. Charlie always kept them focused and energised and always demanded they kept finding new ways of making sure their customers were delighted with their service and the company. Tom could see that some thought was occupying her, so he waited until she seemed to refocus on him before continuing.

'All companies start off small – and they are usually begun by an entrepreneur who fits this mould. Remember Apple and Ford, and what about General Electric? It is now one of the biggest companies in the world and it was started by Thomas Edison, the original entrepreneur whose idea it was. What you have in these situations is a team obsessed with creating a company and focusing on cash, customers and creating innovative products or services to fix the customer's problems. As you may only have a few customers, you need to look after them, work with them and help them achieve their own goals in their own company. From what you've told me that was also what Charlie's genius was, because he knew that those customers could have gone anywhere and most likely did not need to take the risk of doing business with a small start-up. However, there clearly would have been something about this particular small start-up that made the customer believe they could trust them.'

Lucy again had a flashback to how enthusiastic their customers had been about the company in the early days and wanted to let Tom know what it had felt like then.

'It's true; everybody really loved working with Charlie, not just the staff but the customers as well. I have never thought about it before, but you're right, they saw something in him that made them trust him, and that encouraged loyalty towards him.'

Tom could see she was really starting to get a clear picture of what the critical differences were between Amroze then, and now. 'That's exactly right. That's why I say that was Charlie's genius because he knew how important customers are and evidently he passed this on to you, too. What you knew back then was that as an entrepreneurial team you needed to treat your customers like royalty and really look after them. Without them, you wouldn't have a business, and it's obvious that if you love the products or services you are delivering, then why would you not love the person who bought them?'

The idea of loving some of the more difficult customers certainly gave Lucy cause for thought, but she could see what Tom was getting at and it suddenly didn't seem too impossible to get back to that original state of drive and focus that she had experienced when she first joined the company. Checking that she was still with him, Tom wound up what he wanted to tell her. 'There is a lot more to say on that subject, but we won't get into that now. I just want to show you what happens in the next part of this cyclical process I have been describing to you.' As he spoke his phone rang, and he excused himself as he checked it. 'Lucy, I'm sorry but

I really need to take this call. It won't take more than a few minutes. Do you mind?'

Lucy certainly didn't mind, in fact she needed a few minutes to catch up on all the things he had already told her.

Chapter 2b

Lucy's thoughts kept going back to Charlie. She hadn't realized how much more fun life had been back then. Examining it now, all these years later, she knew it was the energy, commitment and passion that were missing. Now it was more about processes than people, and if she was honest it had been that way for some time. Tom finished his call and tried to pick up the thread of his thoughts again.

'Now, where was I? Right, let's talk about the next stage of this cyclical process I was describing. Over time your small entrepreneurial company gets bigger, it takes on more staff and those people were not there at the start, so they have a slightly different attachment to the company. The company continues to grow and as it gets bigger there is a need for more capital to maintain that growth. It is around this time that the company changes, when significant levels of external capital come into the business.'

He checked again to make sure she was keeping up with him and when he saw her fingers relax on her pen as she looked up, he went on.

'Lucy, your company is typical in that its problems started when it floated on the stock market because then it was no longer a private company owned by the entrepreneur, but a public company owned by the shareholders and those who invest in it. What they want is a return on their money and they tend to have high expectations for their investment. With financial markets, there is a pressing need for short term financial results and for the company to show how well it is doing. When investors can see good results they have confidence in the company and that drives demand for the shares, and forces the share price up.

'In theory, this means everyone is a winner. But in practice, it isn't because by now the original entrepreneur, Charlie in your case, will most likely have either left the company willingly or been removed because they have no experience of running a public company. Now a professional CEO and a team of managers come in, but out goes the passion and in comes the processes along with a whole new language called "corporate speak". Your new employees only know "corporate speak" and suddenly the mantra of customer and cash is lost. The focus is – as you said – on short term share price. The irony here is that in the long term, you can only maximize the share price by ultimately focusing on customers and cash, back to the basic premise of when the company was formed. Sadly this key element gets lost, especially in the years after the initial stock market listing when the company is awash with investors' money. Being cash rich all of a sudden means the company does not need to worry too much about getting new customers to generate cash to pay the wages and so inevitably the company becomes complacent. Does this sound familiar?'

Lucy was recalling her thoughts from the previous day about how the company had changed once it became public, so she replied unhesitatingly and with conviction. 'Yes it does. Everything you have said relates to Amroze specifically.'

Tom shrugged but he wasn't actually disagreeing with her. 'It applies to Amroze but it is true for just about any other company.'

Lucy was sure she could almost see the way forward, but she still needed to nail it down. 'So, what is the answer?' she asked him in an almost challenging tone.

'As I said before, I think you will find there can only be one answer. You have got to get back to what made your company great in the first place. Reignite the entrepreneurial spirit that Charlie initially brought to the company and that everyone there responded to. All the ingredients that made the company successful in the first place still hold true as it gets bigger, but what happens is that they get pushed aside and the new management don't pay them the attention they need and deserve. Everyone associated with Amroze has to believe in it and that is where you have to begin.'

Privately, Lucy thought that he was undoubtedly right, but Charlie was long gone and there were now few in the company like her, who had been there since the beginning. She tried to express her misgivings to Tom without sounding negative. 'I appreciate what you are saying and I really want to bring that spirit back, but we don't have Charlie or his influence around any more. I do, though, have high hopes that

Stephen will bring some of that spirit back. I need concrete facts to give him and I am not sure how to proceed or what will be the most effective way forward.'

Tom heard both conviction and doubt in her voice. She certainly had faith in Stephen but sounded unsure about the people in the company overall, though he could see she was willing to give it a try. Tom decided it was time to give her a bit of confidence to get the project off to a good start.

'The fact you already know Stephen gives you a heads up on how he will operate. It's clear you understand the fundamental importance of getting back to the mantra of customers and cash. Start there and find out where that isn't happening, and why. I can guarantee that the answer to turning your company around will already be within the company itself. Once you have had a couple of meetings with people then I'll happily bounce some ideas around with you and help you unpick what you've been told by them. You must be willing to really dig deep in order to be absolutely sure you understand what is and isn't working. Without doing that you certainly won't be able to come to a true or accurate conclusion that everybody will believe in and buy into.'

Lucy took that on board, but had one further question for him. 'OK, I agree with what you have said, I can see we have become too comfortable, and although it's a relief to know it's not just us going through these sorts of growing pains or cycles I still need to get to the bottom of why it's happening to us now. I will speak to the staff, but do you want me to speak to some customers as well?'

Tom's reply was emphatic. 'Yes, I do and make that a priority because you really need to know what your customers believe about Amroze. That is a key level of belief that I talked to you about, and we will go deeper into how that works when you have spoken with them. I think I know what they will say, but I want you to hear it for yourself. You and I will be in touch by phone regularly, but this is the best way for you to really understand what is going on.'

Lucy nodded. 'It's fine by me. When shall we speak?'

'Let's talk by phone after you meet with some customers and you can give me your observations. Remember what Charlie said, "it's all about customers and cash". That is the best place to start, because if your customers are not happy, then you really do have problems! Go and really listen to what they have to say, oh and find out if they still love you!' He got up from the couch and said goodbye to her, but Lucy decided to stay a little longer. She wanted the opportunity to sit quietly, read through her notes and make a shortlist of the key points she had learned from Tom. Who to meet first? Well, Tom had suggested she start with the customers, so that was easy to arrange, but at the idea of asking whether they still loved Amroze, she shook her head. That was certainly going to get her some interesting replies!

TOM'S ADVICE

- Business is predictable. All companies go through growing pains with the transition from start-up to mature company, or mature company to market leader
- Companies are started by entrepreneurs with passion, belief, desire and drive
- Entrepreneurs inspire their teams to believe and achieve impossible outcomes against all odds
- As companies grow, the entrepreneurial mindset is lost and replaced with an employee or corporate mindset
- In mature companies passion is often replaced by processes and the focus on customers and cash is replaced by a focus on share price
- Companies must get back to their entrepreneurial roots to survive in changing markets.

Chapter Three

Lucy wasted no time in taking Tom's advice and headed straight back to the office to set up a series of meetings with some of their customers for the next day. She brought up a list of their key customers on her computer and identified a random sample, from major accounts to small independent businesses, and printed off a list to start calling straight away. Although it was getting late in the day, she reached a couple of local customers who agreed to meet her in person within a couple of days and she was able to schedule phone calls with a few more over the same period. Satisfied she had made a good start, she had one final call to make before she headed home. It was important to start getting input and feedback from the various departments in the company as soon as possible and again she made a list of the key areas and didn't need much thought before deciding to go first to the sales and marketing department as she knew they would have plenty to say! Picking up the phone again she called Malcolm Thomas, the sales director, but he had already left for the day so she left a message saying she would appreciate some time with him later in the week, together with a few of his sales team. She wondered who he would elect to bring to the meeting, as she already knew quite a few of them, and wanted to get a representative sample of the different opinions in the department. Thinking about it, she decided that when he rang to set up the meeting she would make a specific request for a few of the people she thought would have a strong contribution to make.

At home later that evening she was thinking about the task she was faced with. Glancing at her notes, it struck her again that although she thought the situation at Amroze

Technology was unique, Tom had been very persuasive in his comments that all companies experience these very same issues at some time in their existence. She noted that heavily underlined phrase he had used several times, where he had talked about how the company had to 'reignite its entrepreneurial spirit'. Although not conscious of it, this brought a slight frown to her face as Lucy knew full well that the word 'entrepreneur' was not a popular one in Amroze Technology. As she thought about it, she recalled standing by the lift waiting to go up to her office and overhearing a conversation with the last CEO talking to the CFO and saying that the last thing the company needed was the staff becoming entrepreneurial. The words that had really struck her were when the CEO had said 'We have no time for risk in this company, we have shareholders to look after' and then the two men had got into the lift and she had heard no more. Lucy wondered what Tom would have to say about that view, but was fairly sure he would disagree – in fact she realized she wasn't convinced by it herself.

The following morning she didn't go straight to the office, but stopped first at one of the local companies she had managed to set up meetings with the day before. They were on a small industrial estate on the edge of town and it was only a short journey from her home. Driving round the park, looking for them amongst all the uniform grey buildings she realized that she felt quite nervous and apprehensive. She stopped the car for a few moments to think things through as this was not the ideal state to be going to see a customer in. They were a new customer to Amroze and although she had never had any previous contact with them she still wanted to make a good impression. Lucy had been into hundreds of customers' sites over the years when she helped implement the technology or even when she worked in sales, and thinking about it she realized that this was the source of her unease. Here she was going in under a completely different guise. She wasn't here to fix a technology problem; she wanted the MD to give her feedback on Amroze Technology's performance for them, and to find out what they really thought of the company. Having realized what her discomfort was all about, she steadied herself, took a deep breath and drove on and by the time she had parked in the visitors' bay she was a lot calmer.

Lucy was immediately shown through to a conference room where coffee was laid out. Three people were already seated around a boardroom table, casually chatting while they waited to meet her. David Watson, the smartly dressed MD, stood up to shake Lucy's hand and although he was perfectly pleasant she didn't get any real feeling of welcome. He seemed to be rather reserved and she hoped that it wasn't down to her visit. It was with a bit of relief she saw the two younger people in the room who were more casually dressed and relaxed. He introduced them as Mike Gill and Kerry Starr and said he hoped she didn't mind them joining the meeting. Wryly he commented that while he got the end results, they were the ones who used the software that Amroze Technology had developed and so their comments might be more constructive.

Lucy said she was delighted because she wanted to get as much input as possible and the more points of view she got, the better it was for everyone. Lucy was offered coffee, and when everyone was settled she left it to David to start the meeting. He repeated why Lucy had come, and that they were very pleased to have the opportunity to give some feedback. Lucy smiled encouragingly, but wondered just what was going to come out. David asked Mike to take the lead on how they found dealing with Amroze Technology and using its software and, as he opened a folder in front of him, Lucy could see that it was full of documents and handwritten notes.

He was a man of about her own age, confident and yet slightly apologetic, as if he was about to break bad news. From his manner and his body language it was immediately clear that Mike's feedback was going to be a lot less than positive. He shuffled the papers for a moment, and then finally looked across the table at her. His eyes were sympathetic, but his words were hard to hear.

'It seems to me that nobody really cares at Amroze Technology. I would have thought that you would value your customers a bit more, but I'm sorry to say it seems to me that we almost seem to be an after thought.' He checked to see how she was taking it, and reassured by her calm manner, he continued. 'I was actually involved in the original decision to buy your software, along with David of course, and at the time your sales guy could not have been more accommodating. He promised us the earth and we definitely thought that this software would really change our business and help us grow. It was an important decision on our part because I know this was a major investment for us, but it just hasn't delivered.'

Lucy tried to keep her emotions in check while she wrote down Mike's comments, and hoped none of the others could see how much impact his words had on her. Mike still had more to say.

'Now, it's a completely different story. From initially being in constant contact with us over what we needed, we now never hear from your sales guy at all. When we had problems we had to chase him for a response and when we finally got hold of him he told us that our problems were an implementation or support issue and had nothing to do with him. Now, it seems we spend more time on the phone to your support team than anyone else and that's not the end of the problem. When we call your support department we just get passed from pillar to post with nobody really accepting responsibility. We have a list of outstanding issues, but we are really struggling to get these fixed or find the right person to help us. I am so unhappy with the situation that I have recommended to David that he does not pay your next invoice until these problems are fixed, because that seems to be the only way to get through to you.'

Lucy kept writing, and wondered why the upright leather chair she had first sat in had seemed so comfortable when now what she really wanted was something she could sink down into out of sight.

'And to make matters worse, I had a call from your PR department just a few days ago asking if you could write a feature about us for your latest press release. You can guess what I said to her.' He threw up his hands in despair as he asked Lucy, 'Tell me, doesn't anybody ever talk to each other in your company?'

As Mike sat back in his chair, clearly having finished his complaint for the time being, David stepped in.

'Lucy, as you can see, we are not a happy customer at the moment. If anybody asked me if they should buy from Amroze Technology, I would have to say no to them. Your products are not working for us and your customer care is shocking and that is just not acceptable.'

Lucy could hardly bear to hear what Kerry had to say, and only hoped it wasn't going to be more of the same. However, although Kerry tried to soften it by smiling a lot, what she actually said was perhaps even worse than Mike's comments. He had complained about the aftercare but she made it clear that her problem was more fundamental. She was struggling to work with the software and in fact, their old software system was easier, more reliable and less time consuming to use. She put it even more strongly than that, she felt that the Amroze salesman had sold the wrong system for their needs.

Lucy's coffee had sat untouched throughout the meeting, and as she swallowed the now-cold drink she realized that she had only a few minutes left before she had to leave to see another customer across town. However, it was important to her to reassure them that she had heard what they said.

'I must apologize because I have to go now, but I promise you that things are going to be different. I am truly sorry to hear about these problems, but that is why I came; to dis- cover exactly what is going wrong, and I'm here specifically at the request of our new CEO, Stephen Fox, who takes over in a few weeks' time. He wants to have all the relevant information so we can make the appropriate changes to improve in the areas you have mentioned you are unhappy with. I promise we are taking it very seriously indeed. I am grateful that you took the time to give me this feedback and I will personally make sure that the specific issues you mentioned are addressed by the relevant people.'

She was in a thoughtful mood as she set off for her next meeting, and was definitely hoping that this one would turn out better. There was a chance it might, as this company had been a customer almost since Amroze Technology was formed, and she had implemented their first systems many years ago and so knew the director she was meeting from that time. Duncan Corelli greeted Lucy as if they had only seen each other a few weeks ago, and seeing him was like meeting an old friend. It was actually quite a few years since she had dealt with his account and so they spent some time catching up. Duncan was interested to hear all about her progress, particularly her work overseas and was delighted to hear about her completing her MBA, something they had often talked about her doing. She felt confident that here was somebody she knew would be able to give her some honest feedback about the company, and how it was doing right now in meeting customers' needs.

As they reached the natural end of their catch up, Lucy felt comfortable enough to ask Duncan for his feedback. 'Are you really sure you want to hear this?' Lucy's heart sank, she had hoped this time would be better but it was beginning to sound like it might be more of the same.

'Come on Duncan, you know I can take it. Let's hear the worst.'

He was happy to help her and started by reminiscing about how it was in the old days when Charlie and the original team were there. 'Those were good days, Lucy, because back then your company would do absolutely anything for me and valued me as a customer. They really understood that the only reason I had bought the software in the first place was because it fixed my specific business problem and I really believed that the software would make my company more successful. It was a clear decision, the information the software delivered and the processing of it helped me make better decisions, which helped my company to grow. Charlie understood that, and for quite some time so did the rest of the people at Amroze.'

Lucy leaned forward; she could tell from that last remark that Duncan was very clear about what had gone wrong. He pointed out that they had been a loyal customer to Amroze, buying a lot of new software from them and paying ongoing support costs. His normally friendly and open expression had taken on a more serious look and he paused before continuing.

'You know, it's good timing that you called me because we are seriously thinking about changing our software supplier. Technology has moved on quite a bit in recent years and we don't believe in here that your software has kept up with what's cutting edge out there. We think we are missing out on some vital management information that would help our own company grow, but without access to that information, we are being held back.' He looked enquiringly at Lucy, waiting for a response; she wanted to be sure she understood exactly what the core problem was so asked a question that ought to clarify it.

'Have you requested that our developers take a look at providing this information for you and build it into our software?' Duncan's rather disbelieving look provided the answer but he gave it to her anyway.

'Have I? I don't know how many times I've asked but nothing ever gets done; that's why we're looking at new software.' He opened a drawer in his desk and pulled out a folder which he opened for her to look at. 'I have the brochures right here. I know it is not a cheap alternative to switch software, but I think I'm losing money without this new information so it will be cheaper in the long run. Also, things have moved on in this area, and, to tell the truth, your system is quite expensive to maintain. I think I could get my overall lifetime costs down and make a real return on any new investment in just a matter of months.' Lucy was looking at the brochures in the folder as he spoke, and they were all from Amroze Technology's main competitors. Duncan gestured to the folder and continued. 'Of course it's a pain to change software, but what can I do? Amroze Technology isn't helping me and my requests for help have fallen on deaf ears. I know if Charlie was here, or the original team, that would not be the case, but I am tired of having to chase your guys to get any answers. That's why I have really lost confidence in Amroze Technology and I think it could be time to change. I am sorry Lucy, but from where I stand Amroze just doesn't care any more about me or my business. They are increasingly unhelpful and certainly take me for granted, and I won't put up with it anymore.'

Lucy nodded and closed the folder to hand back to him. Although they spoke for a few more minutes, it was really the same message as she had been given at her previous customer visit. There was just no real customer care, and as before she repeated the same message and promised to follow this up with the new CEO. Duncan was an important customer, and she didn't want the relationship damaged any further so she also promised to ask Stephen to personally call him just as soon as he arrived at Amroze Technology. She had no doubt that Stephen would be happy to do it as he knew, as Lucy did, that losing a customer means losing thousands in recurring revenues each year. As Duncan's company was one of their biggest customers it meant hundreds of thousands in revenue at stake and the company simply could not afford to lose this regular revenue stream.

Normally, Lucy always looked forward to meeting customers but this had not turned out as well as she had hoped. She knew things were not right in the company, but she hadn't anticipated this level of dissatisfaction. Once back in the office she tried to maintain a positive attitude and began the round of customer phone calls she had set up. However, by late afternoon it was obvious that things were much worse than she had imagined. In fact, by the last phone call she could have done both parts of the dialogue all by herself as she was getting so used to hearing it. The complaints were always the same: lack of customer care from Amroze Technology, lack of responsibility, nobody listening to the customer, nobody talking to each other at Amroze Technology, being passed from pillar to post. In short, customers' problems were going unresolved, the software did not work, and they were getting conflicting messages from sales people who would say one thing and then do another.

Whichever way she looked at it, she was not hearing good news, unless you counted the customer who told Lucy how he had made some serious money when he bought shares in Amroze Technology some years ago and sold them a while later at a profit. This man was torn, because, as he explained to her, he kept an eye on Amroze's shares price and as it was now so low, he wondered if he should invest again and maybe make another good profit. However, as a user of the software, and having experience of dealing with the company, he kept thinking better of the idea. He had been sympathetic, but very clear that right now he did not have the confidence to make the investment again in Amroze Technology.

Lucy finished off the phone call feeling she could not take any more bad news. Glancing at her watch, she had time for a coffee and to get her notes in order from all her customer interviews before she was due to speak with Tom at the end of the day. Although she had more customer interviews scheduled for the next few weeks, they had agreed to schedule a call for today to see what the initial tone of the customer meetings was like. She grabbed a coffee and then back at her desk she started a preliminary list of questions that she hoped Tom could help her answer.

She gave the list a quick once over to fix it in her mind before she rang him promptly at 5.30pm. After a few moments exchanging pleasantries, she outlined the devastating nature of the feedback to him and she was quite surprised that he wasn't fazed by it at all. When she initially got the negative feedback from the clients she had been upset to hear it, but Tom was very calm and actually quite reassuring. 'If it's a mentor's job to make me feel better, he has certainly got the right approach,' was her immediate reaction as he told her that this response from customers showed something very typical of many companies like Amroze who were in this part of their growth cycle. Reassured she might be, but Lucy still wanted to know 'why' and knowing it was true of many companies didn't answer the question for her.

'What specifically went so wrong with Amroze then?' she asked him, and his reply was short and to the point.

'In a word: complacency. The company became complacent, you took your customer for granted and took your eye off the very thing you mentioned yesterday – customers and cash.' Lucy had her notebook right next to the phone, and started jotting down his comments. She couldn't believe she had only met Tom 24 hours ago, and yet she already completely trusted his views and knew she was on the right track so she listened carefully to what he was telling her.

'From what you have told me, your customers are not happy and some are even considering switching to one of your competitors. What do you think that will do to your cash flow?' Lucy had no problem with that simple question and promptly responded 'Well, reduce it, of course.' Tom nodded in agreement.

'OK, so why do you think they want to go to one of your competitors?'

This wasn't such a simple question and she glanced down at her notes as she thought it through. 'Because, I suspect they believe they will get a better product and service from them.'

'Spot on. You have said the magic words, "THEY BELIEVE." Lucy, in my view, business is all about belief. In fact I would go further and say that life is all about belief. All of us human beings (and that includes your customers) will not do anything that we do not believe in. Or perhaps I should say – we will not make a major decision that we do not believe in.' He left a pause and although Lucy was still thinking about the obvious but unthought-of idea that customers were human beings she could see immediately where he was headed.

'You mean major decisions like buying expensive software,' and smiled to herself as he agreed.

'Your customers are losing belief in your company; it's as simple as that. From your meetings and conversations today it is obvious that your customers' belief in you is ebbing away. You have witnessed with your own eyes and ears that they do not believe you care, they do not believe your software will fix their problems, or indeed that you will fix the software that you have sold them that does not work. They do not believe your employees talk to each other and they do not believe the promises your salesmen have made to them – in short, they do not believe in you. Even the customer who had invested in your company and made some money on your rising share price will not invest again as he does not believe. Truly, belief is everything because without it your customers do not trust you and if they don't trust you why would they want to go on working with you?'

From the silence that had greeted his last remarks, Tom could sense this was a shock to Lucy as she clearly had not thought of things that way. He helped her out by offering a couple of other examples from the business world, which would make him more certain she fully understood the importance of belief.

'Lucy, I suggested we met yesterday at the airport's conference centre because I had just flown in from out of town. Have you ever been on a plane?'

'Do you know anyone who hasn't?' was her immediate thought. It seemed an odd question to ask as he knew she had travelled pretty much around the world for Amroze. In fact, she had been bitten by the travel bug at university and welcomed any opportunity to go somewhere new. Lucy would hop on a plane in a heartbeat, but she guessed he must have a good reason for asking. She settled for making an affirmative 'uh-huh' and waited for his response.

Tom sounded amused as if he knew she thought it was a dumb question but was humouring him. 'Well, have you ever thought about what flying really involves? It is an amazing thing to get to grips with, that we are suspended above the earth in a tin box. We sit calmly in that aeroplane, take off, defy gravity and land safely at our destination. When you think about it, it is a truly mind-boggling concept to accept. In many ways it is unbelievable, but we do it now almost without thinking about it. Now, if we didn't believe we would take off and land safely at our destination we would not do it'. Lucy who truthfully never gave the idea of flying a second thought, was intrigued by the idea and the more she thought about it the more she could see that belief was at the heart of her being able to take flying for granted.

Satisfied she had understood him, Tom pressed home the point. 'Now tell me this. Would you choose to fly with an airline with a poor safety record; that did not look after you as a customer; who had a reputation for losing its passengers' luggage and had old and out-of-date aircrafts? Plus, the final insult, they had higher prices than their competitors!'

'Of course not. To use your belief analogy, I would not believe they would get me there safely, or on time, or that they would not lose my luggage or that I was getting good value for money.' She could sense that Tom was smiling at her.

'So in short – you say you would not believe in them?'

Lucy was getting a bit tired of this game, but she went along with it. 'That's right' she agreed, but Tom wanted to make it even clearer.

'How about this example? When you vote in an election, who do you vote for?' Lucy wasn't sure this wasn't another trick question, but her answer came quickly enough.

'That's simple, I vote for the party and leader who I most believe will make a difference to the country. OK, I think I know where you are taking this one.'

'Yes, indeed.' Tom agreed with her. 'Politics is the ultimate show of belief. People are free to vote for whoever they want, but generally they will only vote for who they believe will be the best leader and party. You put your vote behind someone you believe will do their best for schools, hospitals and for your own family and their needs. If you do not believe in the politician, you will use your vote to show it.'

Thinking of some spectacular election crashes in recent years, Lucy had to admit he was right. Once belief was withdrawn, so was the commitment to that person or party. Tom now wanted her to relate it specifically to her own problems at Amroze.

'Ultimately, success in business is about belief – and to start with your customers have to believe. I want you to remember the phrase "THEY BELIEVE". I want you to know that "they must always believe" and "they" are the customer. In politics, you and I are the customer and it is the job of the political parties to ensure that we believe in them. Primarily that is what they are looking for – our belief.

'Your customers also want to believe and you have a lot of ground to make up here. Don't worry, it will all become clear as we speak over the coming weeks, but the key concept I want you to start building Amroze Technology's new foundation on is that without the belief of your customers, you will always struggle in your business.'

Lucy absorbed the importance of the idea Tom was talking to her about. Of course, she had always known how important the customer was, but what she could now see was that it wasn't something you could rely on. You had to keep working on it. Tom had been silent for a few seconds as he realized she was taking it all in and then he went on.

'You need to realize that you have to get their belief back and there is only one way to do that. You must start putting your customer first again. From what you have told me, in recent years your company has become too complacent and focused on itself and it seems to me that many of your staff have lost the connection between the customer and cash. This most likely happened as you expanded and got bigger; I suspect that many of your staff go for days, weeks or months without even thinking about why a customer would want to buy from you and what they could personally do to make sure the customer still believes.'

Lucy thought she had got it, but one thing still niggled at her. 'So this happens to most companies at some point?' Tom laughed out loud.

'Not to the smart ones! Yes, to many, but if you want an example of someone who absolutely walked his talk on the customer being king, then what about Sam Walton? He was the entrepreneur behind Wal-Mart and if he was alive today he would be the richest man in the world, twice as rich as Bill Gates.'

'I'm guessing Sam's philosophy was to put the customer first?' Lucy joked as she wrote the phrase in large letters in her notebook.

'Yes, absolutely right. He put the customers first, and they believed in Sam Walton and they helped him create a great business. All because they believed!'

Lucy underlined the phrase and she and Tom ended their conversation with a reminder of their meeting the following week. Lucy closed her notebook and realized that she was starting to feel more optimistic. It didn't feel like uncharted territory because Tom was definitely giving her a map and pointing out the signposts. The journey was well under way!

TOM'S ADVICE

- Belief is everything
- Customers and prospects want to believe in your company — it is your job to make sure THEY BELIEVE
- It is all too easy to become complacent and take your customers for granted
- If customers do not believe or are taken for granted, they will go elsewhere (to competitor companies who they do believe in)
- Human nature says we will not do anything we do not believe in. The only reason a decision maker will not choose your product, service or company is because they do not believe in you and your offer
- Think Sam Walton! If Sam was alive today, he would be twice as rich as Bill Gates. Sam Walton always put his customers' interests first and made sure he gave them something to believe in (i.e. great products at great prices) and he made sure they came back as repeat customers for life.

Chapter Four

Lucy had spent the previous evening at a restaurant with friends and was feeling more relaxed and focused for having taken the evening off. She had absorbed the blow from the customers' comments and was looking forward to spending time with Amroze Technology's own sales and marketing team. After all, they were the people who were responsible for generating new customers and they, she hoped, would be able to shed some light on the reasons customers were so dissatisfied. Feeling more confident of a good outcome, she waved an enthusiastic good morning to Claire the receptionist as she headed towards the stairs to her office. After checking there were no urgent messages to deal with, she headed on down the corridor for her first meeting of the day with Malcolm Thomas, Amroze's Executive Sales Director. With overall responsibility for worldwide sales and a team of 250 international sales people reporting to him all over the world she felt confident that, with a little probing, he could give her some of the answers she was looking for after speaking to the customers yesterday.

His secretary motioned for her to go through, but warned he was just finishing off a phone call. She hadn't been here before and it was clear that his office reflected his status and importance in the company. Unlike her new mini-office that she had tried to brighten up with plants and photos, this room had double-wall large picture windows and impressive leather chairs around a large circular mahogany table. Lucy settled back and glanced round at the various certificates on the wall as she waited. Malcolm Thomas noticed her looking, and signalled he was winding up his call. He joined her at the table and she began by outlining again the project the incoming

CEO had given her and the importance of having a workable strategy to present to him as soon as he arrived. She could see he was curious as to why she wanted to speak with him specifically, but he just smiled and nodded. 'Studying me first to find out what I want before he gives me a response – this guy must be a good salesman!' she thought to herself as she began recapping some of the comments from her meetings with the customers she had met with and spoken to the previous day. Although she pointed out that she still had many other customers to meet with, the initial feedback had been so strong that she wanted to talk to him before meeting any of the others. She paused, but he just nodded and waited for her to elaborate. Lucy didn't need to check her notes; she had got the message so clearly from the customers, so she succinctly laid their comments out for him. She kept her voice neutral, but put strong emphasis on the fact that they were not satisfied with the level of service from Amroze Technology and they did not feel valued as customers.

He listened in silence, and Lucy wasn't sure how he was taking her comments. There had been criticism from the customers about how the sales staff had over-promised and then not delivered on the aftercare and she could see that he was carefully considering his response. He was still relaxed, but looking a bit more wary. 'Please don't let him get defensive on me, I just want him to shed some light on what the problem is,' was her thought as she watched what appeared to be him mentally running through a list in his head. When he finally spoke he kept his voice as neutral as hers had been.

'Lucy, let me start by framing the situation we are faced with because what you have to look at is the big picture here.

In sales, we are responsible for generating new business, for getting new customers through the door – and also getting more business from our existing customers. That is our sole responsibility and as a company that is quoted on the stock market, we have huge expectations set upon us to meet our sales targets. Now these targets are to a large degree set by the market and those analysts who follow our company. If we do not reach our sales targets on a quarter-by-quarter basis, then investors lose confidence in us and the share price falls.' Lucy leaned forward to ask a question, but he held up a hand to stop her. He clearly didn't want her to interrupt, and he intended to make his point clear.

'Now you will most likely have stock options in Amroze Technology so you don't want that. Investors certainly don't want that – nobody wants to see the share price go down. So making sure we reach our sales targets is imperative – at all costs.' Lucy did not like the sound of that and this time she didn't let him stop her interrupting.

'Even if that means having unhappy customers?'

He gave her an irritated look. 'Clearly we want happy customers, because happy customers come back and buy from us again and again. It is much more cost effective for us to get business from an existing customer rather than trying to find a new one, but at the end of the day, hitting sales targets is what it is all about for us.' Satisfied he had explained their position clearly, he looked at her to see if she had any questions.

His single-minded view wasn't a surprise, but she did wonder why he hadn't even asked what the customers' dissatisfaction was all about. It was triggering something that

Tom had said to her, but she couldn't just recall it so she took a moment to mull Malcolm's comments over. Maybe there was another question she could ask that would help explain why some of the customers she had spoken to had been so dissatisfied, although this might be tricky territory. However, she needed to know so took a deep breath. 'Can you tell me how the sales team are paid? Is it a straight salary or do they get part of their package paid as a bonus?' Happily, this didn't seem to bother him.

'Clearly we pay for results so most of the salesperson's package is made up of commission. As soon as they close a sale they receive a bonus, which is a percentage of the overall deal. This way it is clearly in their best interests to sell as much as possible each month and quarter.'

'It's in their interests to sell, but where is their interest in looking after the customer?' The emphasis that Tom had put on really connecting and treating customers well was echoing in her head. With this in mind, she used a roundabout way of finding out just how motivated the team were to see the customer happy.

'So does the sales person have any responsibility for the success of the overall project?' Malcolm shook his head as if bemused by the idea.

'No, of course not. What we want is for our sales team to focus on sales and let the implementation team focus on delivering the project. Once our sales team have done the deal, we get them paid so that motivates them to move on to the next prospect and make sure they hit those sales targets, and keep on hitting them.' It was clear to Lucy that he didn't get her concern, and that for him the meeting was over. 'Look,

I know you asked to you speak with a couple of people on our sales team, but unfortunately neither of the people you requested is actually in today.' Lucy wondered if that was by design, perhaps he thought they might be too outspoken and she definitely had the sense that Malcolm Thomas was not a man who took kindly to criticism. Perhaps it had been a mistake to mention that she had already worked with them. Ah well, no point in getting too disheartened by it. She smiled at Malcolm as he rose and walked back to his desk and dialled a number. 'Ken? I've got Lucy Robinson in my office and she's doing a special project for the new CEO. Can you spare a few minutes to speak with her? Fine, I will send her out.' 'He can't wait to get rid of me,' was Lucy's thought as he replaced the receiver and walked to the door of his office to show her out. 'Ken Chang is a fairly new salesman with the company so he can probably give you a different perspective.' As she headed into the main sales office Lucy knew he hadn't been too happy with the interview and was holding back a bit. She hoped Ken Chang might be more open.

The sales team had a large open-plan office divided into individual cubicles and there were the usual personal touches of family photos, plants and cheerful posters. As she stood looking around a young man peered over the top of the one that was right in the centre of the office. He was in his late twenties and dressed in a sharp navy suit and contrasting tie. He smiled at Lucy and waved her over.

'Hi, Ken Chang – good to meet you.' Lucy shook his hand and glanced round his cubicle, which was extremely tidy with sales target lists pinned carefully to the board and the only decoration a framed photo of a large group of people at what was obviously a formal dinner. Although everyone was in evening dress the group seemed relaxed and at ease with each other and she could see him smiling in the middle of the group as they all raised their glasses to the camera. He nodded towards it, 'That was my leaving party at my last company. They were a great bunch of people.' There didn't seem to be any reason why so far, but Lucy got the feeling that he was not quite as impressed with Amroze. She gestured to the cubicle 'Well, you seem to have been put at the hub of the sales floor, not bad for a new guy!' He laughed and pushed his chair under the desk ready to leave.

'Actually it's the furthest from the coffee machine and the photocopier, I think I get to work my way to the water cooler by degrees! Look, it's a bit crowded here, and I am off on a sales call in 20 minutes so would it be OK for you if we went to the coffee shop downstairs?' Lucy was more than happy to agree as she got the feeling he might be more open if they were not in the office where other people would be able to listen in on their conversation.

Once they were settled at a table with their coffees, Lucy began to tell him about the special project she was working on for the new CEO, Stephen Fox, and she knew she was telling it more clearly with each repetition. He seemed genuinely interested, if a little wary, when she explained that she wanted to get a handle on the state of the company and to understand from someone at the sharp end of the business just how it was for the sales team selling the company's current products and services.

Ken stirred his coffee, and gave a slight shrug, 'Well, I really think that our guys are doing a great job under the circumstances.' Lucy was keen to allay any fears he might have about 'telling tales'.

'Without a doubt, Ken, it's just those "circumstances" that I'm hoping between us all we will be able to improve upon.'

'Hmm, to tell you the truth it is tough at the moment but that's probably not what you want to hear.' Lucy had her notebook on the table between them, and she looked up and nodded encouragingly at him.

'The truth is exactly what I want to hear, and believe me so does Stephen Fox.' He seemed reassured by that and relaxed a little.

'I've only been here for six months, but I've spent many years working in this sector, and with some of your major competitors. It is a real challenge selling our software to our customers and if I am being really honest here I do not feel that we have the best technology or products to offer them.' His emphasis was quiet, but very forceful and Lucy wrote down exactly what he had said as she could see that for him this was the heart of the problem. 'From what I know about Amroze, I'm sure that in the past they were a great company. In fact I know they were because when I was with a certain one of your competitors I was always aware of Amroze and how they were the industry leaders. Mostly it was Amroze we lost out to on major contracts, but I know that's no longer the case. To be honest, I was headhunted into Amroze and presented with a package I couldn't refuse. At the time I knew they weren't doing well but I also optimistically thought I could make a difference.' Lucy privately thought this was exactly the kind of employee that Amroze needed. Ken Chang's normally amiable face now had a frustrated look about it, and Lucy kept quiet as she wanted to let him say his piece without interrupting him.

'Now I am closer to Amroze I can see that the technology is old and no longer meets the customer's needs. So much has changed in a relatively short time frame in our sector and Amroze just haven't kept up in the way that our competitors have. That's why it is a really tough sell because prospects not only have plenty of choice but the competitors usually beat us on price too. I'm not making excuses, but you did ask and this is the reality.'

Lucy felt she was really making headway and everything Ken was saying reinforced what the customers had already told her. She could have left it at that, but it wasn't in Lucy's nature to give up until she felt there was nothing more to be gained, and Amroze's future might depend on her getting all the information she could for Stephen. Maybe she could go a bit deeper and try a different type of question that might uncover something even more useful.

'But you have been successful in selling since you have been here, haven't you?' Ken nodded his agreement but still didn't look too happy.

'Sure I have, but sometimes in order to get a result you have to stretch the truth a little to close the deal. This is a highly competitive market, as I said, so I am sure we are not alone in doing that but sometimes I have had to make some pretty big promises to get the business, and to be honest that doesn't sit right with me. I'm sure you heard from Malcolm about the pressure we are under to hit our sales targets? Well you really do not want to know what happens if we miss them!'

He finished his cup as Lucy jotted down some of the points he had made. She was beginning to understand a little more about the basis for the customer complaints and some of their negative comments about the sales force. Ken Chang had given her a much better understanding of the reality of the sales process than she had got from his boss and she realized that the team were not all on the same page. She could see that because there was so much pressure on the sales team to meet targets set by the financial markets, and because most of their salary was paid in commission, they would do whatever it took to close the deal. Lucy was no fool and could see how this could easily result in Amroze's products and services being oversold, especially given Ken Chang's comments that the technology they now offered was no longer the best in the market. She remembered what Mike Gill had told her yesterday about how the sales person had promised them the earth before the order, but then never delivered on those promises. Ken Chang had just clearly illustrated how and why that had happened to customers just like them.

As Lucy was finishing off writing down Ken's comments she heard him greet a woman who was approaching their table. 'Hi Gracie, are you taking an early coffee break too?' Lucy looked up and recognized Gracie Smith, the marketing director and also smiled a greeting. There had been a few key people in the company that Lucy had left messages for asking for a meeting and hadn't yet heard back from and Gracie Smith was certainly someone she was keen to meet. Ken Chang stood up to make room for her, but she shook her head, explaining she was on her way to a meeting and

was just collecting one of her colleagues. 'In fact, I am haul-
ing him out of here before he gets a chance to eat another
doughnut!' She was a tall woman with a striking profile and
Lucy envied the air of subtle confidence that she carried with
her. Plus, she had a great sense of humour and that was in
short supply in Amroze right now. Gracie acknowledged her
and apologized for not ringing her back. She offered to meet
up that afternoon around 3pm and, with nothing booked in
yet, Lucy happily accepted. Gracie Smith nodded and walked
on to the other side of the café to collect her colleague; as
Lucy watched, he hurriedly wiped sugar from his mouth as he
saw her approaching him. Smiling to herself she turned back
to Ken who was getting ready to leave for his own appointment and thanked him for his time and his honesty. 'I know
we all want the same thing here and what you have told me
has really been helpful. Thank you.' They walked out of the
coffee shop together and Lucy headed back to her office as
Ken walked off towards the car park.

Before her meeting with Gracie Smith that afternoon Lucy
wanted to spend some time reviewing Amroze's marketing
materials and website. 'It's all very well finding out what the
employees think,' was her main thought, 'but just what does
the outside world make of us at the moment?' She wanted
to get a feel for the kind of image Amroze presented so she
went to www.amroze.com. It certainly gave the impression of
a successful company, solid and at the top of the market. She
then turned her attention to their sales materials and annual
reports and again the picture looked good. The photos and
language were positive and extolled the many virtues of
Amroze Technology as a company and a first-rate service

provider for those customers. 'Well, you certainly wouldn't know from any of this that sales are down, staff morale is low, and the customers are not happy,' she thought to herself. To those on the outside all looked well; to those on the inside, however, it seemed to be a different story. Thinking it through, Lucy already knew marketing played a vital part in presenting a successful image of the company to the world, but, just as importantly, it gave customers confidence in selecting Amroze Technology as a supplier.

She heard her stomach protesting, and looking at her watch realized she had spent a couple of hours reviewing and writing notes. It was time for lunch, but there was one more thing she could quickly do to add another piece to the puzzle. Grabbing her coat and bag she walked down the stairs. 'This is the only exercise I am getting,' was her rueful thought as she went into reception. Before going out of the door she went over to the main reception desk. People talk about reception being the real front line, where most people get their initial impression of the company, so maybe it was time to see if that was more than just a piece of PR. It hadn't occurred to her before, but as she approached the desk she noticed just how much activity went on around a reception desk. A mail messenger waiting for a signature, several people enquiring about appointments and in the middle of all of it the receptionist was answering the phone as well. 'She has got to know what's going on, she comes into contact with more people than anyone else in the company,' was Lucy's thought as she saw the dark head of Claire, the senior receptionist. She knew Claire had been with Amroze a number of years, and was doing her usual incredible job of multi-tasking. Lucy watched until there seemed to be a slight lull, and when Claire looked up with a slightly distracted smile she began gently quizzing her about what she saw as the current state of affairs in the company. As Claire continued to handle the demands on her attention, Lucy jotted down the key points that she spoke about, and although there were plenty of interruptions to their conversation, Lucy knew she had definitely made a good decision to include reception as part of her project.

When she felt that there was no more to be found out from Claire, Lucy headed out of the building and looked for a quiet place for lunch. She chose a little local café and sat and looked at her notes while she waited for the waitress to come over. Claire had definitely been a mine of information and there were a few comments that Lucy had highlighted. She had been interested in whether Claire had felt her job had changed at all in the last couple of years and had received a clear indication that it had.

'It's nothing drastic, but definitely there have been a lot more phone calls from irate customers. Once, it was really unusual to get one at all, now there are at least a couple a week. I get to know a lot of the customers over the years, and I am pretty good at recognizing voices. People like it when you remember their name and they have always been really polite to me.' She smiled and turned away to deal with a visitor who needed a badge to get into the building. When she turned back, Lucy could see that she had been thinking about what she had just told her. 'You know, I hadn't thought about it until you asked, but I have to deal with more people who are not exactly rude, but are impatient and annoyed.

Not with me, most of them say "I know it's not your fault", but if I can't get hold of a representative because there is no one available then I have to deal with it.' This had intrigued Lucy and she wanted more details and although Claire was reluctant to name the culprits she was willing to tell her that the main problem lay with the support department. Claire was quick to point out that she knew it wasn't entirely their fault as they were really just mopping up other people's problems.

'It started when everybody got voicemail. I know it was meant to save time and irritation when you couldn't get hold of someone, but in fact it had the reverse effect. Personally, I think the support people leave their phones permanently switched to voicemail because they virtually never pick up their phones no matter what time of the day I try to put calls through. If you want my honest opinion, they don't want to speak to the customers because they know they are going to start hassling them. Please don't think I am blaming them, I know they are doing the best they can, and I also know from things they have said that this is a widespread problem throughout the company. It's not just down to them.' This was certainly worrying news, but Lucy wasn't sure how Claire had come to this conclusion. When she asked her, Claire just laughed. 'Because I end up trying to calm the customer down and take really long messages; because they won't leave another one on the voicemail. I know because it's more or less the same message from all the customers: "Why has no one called me back from my previous three messages?" You don't need to be a genius to see that they are not answering their phones because they don't have an answer to give them. Might as well just rip out their extensions and be done with it!' Although she said it with a smile, Lucy knew Claire wasn't entirely joking. In the fifteen minutes she had stood talking to Claire, it was obvious she was really good at her job. Lucy had heard her placating one irate person just while she herself had stood at the desk, but it was also clear that she was getting very disillusioned at having to field so much frustration when it wasn't really her job. Lucy put the notes away and ordered the daily special when the waitress had finally come over to her table. For the next half hour, all she wanted to concentrate on was eating her lunch!

When she got back to the office her first priority before her meeting with Gracie Smith was to contact all the other outstanding department heads that she needed to see by the end of the week. With just under three weeks to give Stephen a report and a recommendation it was vital that she kept the momentum going. Luckily she managed to get hold of most of them and by the time her appointment with marketing came around, Lucy felt she had got a reasonable timetable of meetings set up.

Gracie Smith's office was on the top floor and Lucy grabbed another opportunity to stretch her legs by taking the stairs. She even had time to sit and catch her breath as Gracie's previous meeting was running over. Five minutes later a fairly young team of people filed out of Gracie's office and they brought an air of good humour and energy with them. Must have been a good meeting, Lucy thought as she picked up the buzz of people who liked each other and got on well. As they left, Gracie spotted her and waved her in. Gracie too looked relaxed, and she gestured Lucy towards a couple of sofas that were set an angle in a corner of the room. Unlike Malcolm Thomas's office, this was certainly not the den of a traditionalist. Gracie Smith was a modernist and the space was very light and airy with perspex, chrome and glass everywhere. The paintings on the wall weren't to Lucy's taste; they were bold and impressionistic with strong, vivid splashes of colour, but she had to admit they were a good choice. Looking round, Lucy felt that this office made the statement that Gracie Smith had one of the key positions in the company and she had no problem with letting people see that.

Gracie Smith came and took a seat on the opposite sofa. 'Sorry about that, we are looking at next year's campaigns and it took a little longer than I had anticipated. Are you OK here; would you like some coffee or water?' Lucy shook her head and took out her notebook, ready to make her usual pitch about the project she was doing, but Gracie got in first.

'I know why you are here, in fact everyone in the company is talking about it and I gather that what you want is an overview of what is happening and any concerns I may have. Is that right?' Lucy liked her straightforward approach, and didn't mind at all having to forgo repeating her little speech and just indicated that it was fine for Gracie to continue. 'Well, I don't know how much you actually know about marketing?' Lucy, in the early days of her career at Amroze, had spent quite a lot of time on marketing, but felt it was diplomatic and more useful to just let Gracie give an overview.

'OK, let's just do the quick tour.' Gracie Smith was enthusiastic and knowledgeable and it was a real pleasure to listen to her. 'I am head of Amroze's marketing worldwide and the meeting you just saw breaking up was with my team. Our main priority right now is to see how best to position the company next year. We are affected by lots of elements both internal and external; it's not just what's happening in our industry but what's going on in the world at large that can affect how people see us. We present the "public face" of the company if you like, but we are dependent on key areas like sales, for instance. There is a very strong link between sales and marketing and where we are responsible for creating the brand awareness and desire for Amroze Technology products; it is the job of the sales department to actually close the deals. They need a strong image from marketing in order to successfully close their sales – they need a strong brand image to sell. However, at the moment although the brand itself still counts for a lot, these days we need to do a bit more work to keep us up there.'

Despite her very confident delivery, Gracie was expressing real concern about the strength of the brand and this wasn't something Lucy had heard from anyone else. She wanted to know more, but when she asked for details she could sense that Gracie was a bit reluctant to put it into words. 'Maybe a bit of reinforcement or reassurance is needed. If she thinks I am just telling tales back to the CEO I am not going to get her real opinion on what the problem is,' Lucy thought. So she smiled encouragingly and looked Gracie in the eye.

'Look, what you say to me is in complete confidence. The only people who will know what you say are you, me and the new CEO. He wants to put the company back on track, but to do that he needs information, and he's given me the job of asking the awkward questions so that we can all benefit from what we learn.' Gracie studied her for a second and then relaxed back into the sofa. She slowly moved her head from side to side as if trying to shake the thoughts loose and she spoke in a more considered way than she had before.

'The main problem in my opinion is that the company has been resting too heavily on the heritage of the brand, our history is of being number one and expecting to always be that. In the last couple of years I have become more and more aware that the products have not kept pace with either the market generally, or our customers' expectations in particular.' Her sincerity was obvious and it struck Lucy that this was something she had wanted to say for some time. It had clearly been on her mind long before Lucy had asked for an interview and it felt like this was just the first indication of what she was thinking. There had to be more to come, and there was.

'Over the past few years, there have been a lot of changes in the way our customers do business and in what they need from our technology. If I am honest with you, we have had to be very creative with our marketing to still present a USP (a unique selling point) to our prospects and customers. Of course that's our job and we do it well – I have a great team here but they are getting stretched to the limit. We have to put a lot of creative marketing spin on what we are saying about the company and the products. Sadly, the product development area has not kept up with the customers' needs.' Because she had direct experience of this herself, Lucy encouraged her with what she had learned from the customers yesterday.

'I suspect it is only when they have implemented the systems that the customer really knows if the technology works for them or not.' Gracie threw up her hands in agreement, pleased Lucy got the point. 'Exactly right, and the good news for us is that by then the sale is completed, but the customer may not have got what they needed or wanted.'

'Time for a more risky question,' Lucy thought. 'Do you think we have many satisfied customers?'

Gracie sighed a little while she considered her response. 'I would say that our original customers were very satisfied, but in recent years our customer satisfaction levels have certainly diminished. We used to be able to publish a lot of positive PR about our customers and how they benefited from our software, but in recent years it has been a lot tougher to get those stories.' She remembered the indignation of David Watson when he was approached for a PR story from a company he believed had let him down. She made a quick note of the connection and carried on listening to Gracie. 'I know from talking to Malcolm in sales that being unable to produce "good news" stories definitely has a real knock-on effect on our ability to attract new prospects. They want to read about other happy customers or go and visit other happy customers and, of late, we have struggled to be able to provide those references. I think the sales team suffer significantly because of our lack of reference customers.'

Thinking back to her interview with Malcolm Thomas, Lucy didn't remember him making that point. Lucy had to admire the way that Gracie Smith, without actually coming out and saying so, had established that Amroze Technology's marketing was superior to its products. The research she had done before her meeting with Gracie had shown her that the marketing materials had been updated each year and Lucy had noticed that they had become more and more persuasive without actually being able to say anything new. The sad reality that she was hearing from all sides was that the products themselves had not changed in any major way but their competitors had developed products to meet the changing needs of customers. Amroze had underinvested in its product development, but done a great job on its marketing and branding. Gracie had made it abundantly clear that it was inevitable that sooner or later – and sooner appeared to already be here – there would be a catch-up period when customers realized that the products fell short of the great branding. No matter how good the marketing department was, or how skilled at extolling the products, if the products themselves didn't match up then conflict was inevitable. Time to call it a day and she had got plenty to think about. She needed to look at how to put all Gracie's comments into perspective with those she had already received. Lucy thanked Gracie for her help as she stood up and made a move towards the door. Gracie held out her hand to say goodbye. 'Good luck with it all, Lucy, I know it's a challenging project and I just hope that what we talked about makes a difference.'

'So do I, so do I,' thought Lucy as she headed back to her own office to make her scheduled phone call to Tom.

It had been Tom's suggestion that he and Lucy speak on a regular basis so that he could help her focus on the information she had established during her interviews and get a clearer overview of what was really going on. Hearing his voice on the phone helped her get her thoughts together and she began by recapping her meetings with the sales director and Ken Chang from his sales team. Tom listened in silence and when she expressed her concern about their sole focus on getting short-term sales at the expense of everything else he again repeated his earlier observation when they had first met, that this was a common problem with larger companies who were listed on the stock market. He knew only too well it was the long-term value of the customer that really made the difference.

She remembered him telling her that, but she hadn't expected to see it so graphically illustrated, and when she told him that he gave a short laugh and she could imagine him shaking his head in amusement.

'Acting only with short-term objectives is the real killer of listed companies. Smaller, private companies have only themselves to answer to, but larger listed companies have a whole host of people looking over their shoulders, and breathing down their necks. For a start there are the shareholders, investors and analysts, all of whom keep a close eye on sales results to make sure the company keeps on growing. Investors are generally only interested in growth companies because they want to see their share value go up and that comes from growth in sales and profits. In smaller, private entrepreneurial companies, growth is also vital, but it does not carry the relentless short-term pressure that public quoted companies carry. It is that short-term sales rush that often puts pressure on the sales team to close the deal, no matter what it takes, and that is what can lead to them making promises which simply cannot be supported.'

Lucy was in full agreement with that as it was exactly what she had been told on several occasions. The wisdom Tom was imparting made perfect sense to her and she wrote fast to keep up with what he was saying.

'Let me make a couple of points here. Firstly, you say that customers are not happy, and from what you have told me this is partly a function of the sales process. Secondly, that the products have not kept pace with the market requirements. The key point here is that your customers' needs have changed; they do not want from you the same things they wanted three years, a year, or even six months ago. Just think of all the incredible changes in the world over the past five years in technology, communication and the environment. When you really look at that, it is no wonder that your technology is hard to sell if it is still based on what you did in the past and not on what your customers need right now. Because the world is constantly changing you must have constant and never-ending innovation. Without it you will not meet the needs of your ever-changing customers. Lack of innovation makes it very hard for your products to compete in the marketplace. Ever eaten at McDonalds?'

Though he didn't consciously realize it, Tom was using a technique he had picked up from his old mentor, Michael. Lucy found the abrupt change of subject a bit startling, but didn't want to appear fazed by it.

'More often than I should, they're convenient, and there is always one when you want one. Why?' Although she couldn't see where this was leading, Lucy trusted Tom was about to enlighten her, as indeed he was.

'Yes, that's true, but it didn't prevent them having a very bad few years recently. They allowed themselves to become complacent and sales started to drop off. They didn't react fast enough to the fact that society was changing and being more aware of the health implications associated with fast food. They took their customers for granted, and although their customer loyalty was legendary in the business, they still had to innovate and introduce new healthier products to turn themselves around. Tell me, what is the best sales tool in the world?'

Lucy didn't need to think about this one, as one of her previous bosses had used the phrase like a mantra.

'Personal recommendation, so they tell everyone how great you are and you don't actually have to sell to them; they sell to themselves because someone they trust told them about it.'

'Absolutely, but without having really great products that your customers love and want to rave about, you will struggle to grow as a company.' Tom was really warming to his theme and this was obviously something he felt passionate about. 'Customers must be fans of the company, just as movie stars and rock stars like the Rolling Stones have fans. Customers must have the same attachment. One of the best examples of this is designer clothes. The designers' customers are not just people who buy their products, they are passionate about the clothes and shoes, they have a genuine attachment to them; in other words they are real fans of that designer or brand. If you want to see a demonstration of the highest level of cus-tomer regard, then look at Harley Davidson. Some of their customers even go as far as getting a tattoo of the brand on their body. Now that is true customer love and loyalty.' Lucy had a mind-boggling moment trying to imagine the Amroze Technology logo tattooed onto some of their customers and smiled to herself.

'Customers need to believe in you as a company. That belief is demonstrated when your product becomes a noun or verb. People don't say they're going to vacuum, they say they are going to hoover. They don't surf the net for the answer to a question, they "google" it. Think about it, that is when your customers believe in your company so much that they associate your name with the end action. Look, without customers there would be no business. As a company gets bigger, they can afford to lose customers occasionally and still survive because new customers are still being added. But, and this is the big BUT, sooner or later this will get to the point where more customers are leaving than being added. If you make it your purpose to make your customer happy, then revenue will come over the lifetime of your customer. If you just chase short-term revenue at the expense of customers then you will fail. Only customers provide revenue and they must believe in you.'

Lucy could hear the ring of truth in this and wrote 'THEY BELIEVE' in large letters in her notebook. Starting to adopt Tom's technique of using an example from the commercial world, Lucy ventured, 'You mean companies like Avis who really concentrate on putting the customer first?'

'Absolutely, they are the number two player in the car rental market and had a brilliant advertising slogan saying "because we are number two, we try harder!" Customers could relate to that and believe them. And yes, of course it is all about belief.

Brand value is purely about belief because if a customer believes in it, they will buy it.

'Although not an obvious business, Formula One motor racing is another great example of what I'm talking about regarding constantly striving to stay ahead and having passionate raving fans. The speed of innovation in that industry is relentless. It is a sport run by businesses that have had to become adept at pushing ahead of the competition; constantly looking for the edge, even if that edge is just a fraction of a second. Advances in Formula One are then adopted by leading manufacturers in the wider motoring industry. Formula One lives and breathes the concept of CANI.'

This was a new one on Lucy, and she wasn't sure she had heard him right. 'Can I what?'

'No, not "Can I", CANI stands for "constant and never-ending innovation" and that is just what companies need to be – entrepreneurial and innovative. Product development is entrepreneurial by its very nature; you have to keep moving forward.'

'OK, I get that, but this company doesn't want entrepreneurs. I know I mentioned this to you when we met, but ...'

Tom interrupted her. 'No, your old management didn't want that or at least didn't understand it, but from what I know about Stephen, your new CEO is smart enough to know that all companies need to innovate to survive. I think I made it clear that innovation comes from that entrepreneurial spirit, and it's not an optional extra. If you want your company to be successful, and stay successful, you need the entrepreneurial spirit. Companies can only grow into great companies by expanding their product range, expanding their distribution channels and locations, and by maximizing the lifetime value of customers.

'Let me give you another example. Look at the supermarket giant, Tesco. This is a company started 100 years ago by one man, Jack Cohen, and in recent years they have been brilliant at adapting to meet the changing needs of their customers. Today, customers want local shopping and minimarts in petrol stations, not just large supermarkets. Because the demographic has changed within our society, our needs have changed. Tesco have recognized this and created outlets to reflect that. They have added online shopping and home delivery, because this is what we as customers want. If they had stood still like many of their competitors they would not be the force they are today. Add their international expansion to the mix and you have the perfect model for a growth company. But all the time, they are giving the customer what they want at the price they want. The end result is that their customers believe in Tesco. THEY BELIEVE, and that's what keeps them successful. These things can be turned around. Just keep focusing on the principles of BELIEVE as you continue your interviews and you will see what I am saying in action. Call me again in a few days and good luck.'

Tom ended the call and Lucy had the feeling she needed some quiet time to absorb everything he had told her. She asked the secretary outside to field her calls and then turned to her notebook to make sense of what had happened in her meetings that day.

TOM'S ADVICE

- Many publicly quoted companies can focus too much on short-term profitability rather than on long-term growth. Long-term growth can only come by focusing on the customer
- Only when you focus on the needs of your customer will revenue come. If you chase just short-term revenue, you will not be 100% focused on the most important thing — the life time value (LTV) of your customer
- The world is changing fast, so are the needs of your customers. What they wanted last year is quite likely not what they want this year
- Constant and never-ending innovation (CANI) is critical to keep meeting the needs of your customers
- Failure to meet their changing needs will result in lost belief and ultimately a lost customer and repeat revenue stream to a competitor
- Innovation is an entrepreneurial activity — all companies must therefore keep the entrepreneurial spirit alive. Failure to do so will result in complacency and the company's ultimate demise
- Customers must love you and be fans of your company. If they love your products and services like obsessed raving fans, they will

come back and buy time and time again. Think
designer clothes. Think the Rolling Stones

- The ultimate show of belief is to wear a tattoo
of your brand — or for your company name to
become a noun. Think Harley Davidson (tattoo)
or Google and Hoover (noun and verb).

Chapter Five

Lucy had been given a lot to think about from her phone conversation with Tom and she was eager to push on and get more information so she could start formulating her report for Stephen. When she got to the office the following morning, however, she was disappointed to find a message on her desk saying that her appointment to meet the chief financial officer had to be pushed back due to an urgent unscheduled 'cash flow' meeting he had to attend. Well, she reflected, Tom had mentioned cash flow as being critical to a company's success when they had first met so it was unsurprising that these cash flow meetings were beginning to take place. It was going to be interesting to see what the outcome would be!

Settling down at her desk she prepared to spend the now free morning as productively as she could and pulled up the file detailing the list of customers and members of the sales team that she hadn't managed to speak to yet. It was a good time to get some of the key people at the international sales offices and their worldwide customers. She began making her calls, noting the responses in her trusty notebook and promised herself a cup of coffee after the first six calls. 'Good job I didn't make it a cup of coffee when I got a positive response,' was her wry thought when she had spoken to two of the sales team and four of their customers.

The message was consistent from everybody she spoke to and she was beginning to feel like she was hearing a continuous audio loop. She could sum it up in two short phrases: the customers did not feel valued, and the sales team were struggling to sell uncompetitive products. Though she wasn't sure there was any point in it, she got her coffee and went on to clear most of the list and by the end of the morning her feeling was justified. No matter who she spoke to, the story was the same. She summarized her notes to tell Tom in her next phone call but now wanted to get on and do something different. It was almost lunchtime so she figured some fresh air would do her good and she could grab a sandwich and eat in the park. It was with a sense of relief that she headed out of the building thinking that for at least for an hour she wouldn't have to listen to anyone's negative opinion about Amroze Technology!

As she sat in the sun watching ducks squabbling over a left over piece of bread, she realized that the postponed meeting could be a blessing in disguise as she had not really had enough time to prepare. She hadn't had much contact with Simon Ross, the chief financial officer, but he was a big name in the industry and had come to them from one of their major competitors. Apart from seeing him at company events and reading his name on the bottom of the annual report she had no idea what he was like but figured he would be more likely to listen to her if she had some knowledge of his area, so she decided she would start with getting some background about how others saw the financial status of the company. When she got back to the office, she went online and searched the web to review recent articles about the company and although there were plenty of finance sites to choose from, there wasn't much good news. There had certainly been plenty of coverage about Amroze's performance so there was a lot to read, but it just wasn't very positive.

Amroze Technology, like all other public companies, was tracked closely by several analysts from the major investment banks who gave their opinion whether to buy, sell or hold the stock in the company. Their recommendations were followed closely by other investors who benefited from the time and experience that these experts had in studying the company and usually followed their advice to the letter. Lucy could see that the consensus from the analysts at the moment was to sell and of course, this did little for the share price. Looking at the figures, she could see that the price had plummeted in recent months as Amroze had missed several quarterly sales and profit targets.

Wading through all those reports had taken quite some time, but she checked her watch and she still had an hour before her quick catch up session with Tom so she went on to scan through the internet bulletin boards. Lucy preferred reading these as they were written with the consumer in mind and had actual feedback from investors themselves. This meant the language was much more direct and kept jargon to a minimum so they were much easier to look through and digest than some of the detailed financial reports. 'Not much joy here either,' was her immediate thought as she read through them. There were comments from plenty of disgruntled investors and customers who offered their own opinions as to what was wrong with the company and the message was always the same. It came back time and time again to the quality of their products against their competitors. From an investor's point of view, it was clear that Amroze Technology offered little prospect for growth without some significant change, and nobody was recommending it as a good buy right now.

After a quick call to Tom she decided to call it a day and headed out of the office to continue working at home.

After dinner she sat back and thought through what she had discovered so far. From her conversations with Tom she had begun to adopt a new mindset and was looking at Amroze with new eyes. It was certainly clear that the company had lost its way in recent years and the customers who were originally loyal to Amroze no longer felt that way, in fact some were definitely hostile. The energy and passion that made the company great in the early days had gone and the combination of a lack of innovation and failure to change to meet customers' needs had brought the company to the state it was currently in. 'We can improve our products by really listening to our customers' needs,' reflected Lucy. It sounded so simple and it was frustrating for Lucy that previous CEOs had come and gone without making the connection. 'So what can be done? What are the recommendations?' Lucy felt heartened by the fact that she had a mentor supporting her. With Tom's help she really felt she could crack this. 'Let's hope the decline hasn't gone so far that Stephen won't be able to stop it.' That wasn't a cheerful thought, but there was nothing she could do about it tonight, so she picked up the remote control from the coffee table and settled down to watch television.

Back in the office the next morning she hoped she had done enough preparation to get Simon Ross to open up and share his own insights and what his view of the company currently was. As she walked up the stairs to his office on the next floor she wondered what had tempted him to make the jump to Amroze Technology when he had been chief financial officer with one of their main competitors. Maybe it was the handsome amount of low-priced stock options he would have received when he joined Amroze, and she wondered if he was now regretting it. Still, he must have thought that he could help turn the company around to have considered taking on the role in the first place and she was really looking forward to hearing his views, despite being a little nervous that his seniority would make him less forthcoming.

Simon Ross had one of the neatest offices Lucy had ever seen. There were no papers on his desk, just a calendar, a phone and a computer – if there were any personal items around they must have been locked away behind the doors of the solid wood bookcase that ran the length of two walls and contained matching box files each clearly labelled and in order. Once again she outlined the reason for the meeting and his initial response was positive enough. He had already met Stephen, the new CEO, and thought he was a good choice for the job. Lucy asked him to give her a summary of the company's position as he saw it and once again, out came her trusty notebook.

Simon picked up a pen from beside his phone and she wondered if he was going to take a record of their meeting, but he obviously used it to help him think as he occasionally tapped a rhythm on the desk with it as he spoke. 'It's not good at the moment because our share price is at an all time low; we are being hammered by both the analysts and the markets. In fact, at the price we are at the moment, we are ripe for being taken over, or having to contemplate a merger.'

Lucy was shaken, and briefly remembered her thought of the previous evening whether Stephen would be able to stop the decline, but she certainly hadn't thought things had got quite that bad. His honesty was unexpected but certainly welcome so she kept her questions direct to reflect that. 'Why do you think the share price is so low, Simon?' The pen tapped lightly on the desk as he outlined the problem.

'Well, it is quite simple I'm afraid and comes down to the fact that as our share price went down the investors were unhappy and lost confidence in us. Investors only invest in companies they believe have growth potential and ours clearly don't believe that we have that potential right now. Plus the fact that the analysts who comment on the company have downgraded their rating so again investors are wary.

'It's not surprising really, because we missed our last three earnings forecasts and we cannot hide from the fact that we are not selling enough and that customers are going elsewhere while our investors no longer have faith in our performance.'

Lucy thought back to Tom's philosophy of THEY BELIEVE. 'Does this mean that customers have lost faith in us as well?'

Her comment didn't surprise him; in fact he nodded in agreement. 'I guess you could say that, it is something we clearly need to address. Without growing revenues from new or existing customers we will have major cash flow issues quite soon. That was what my meeting was about yesterday. We now have to secure some short-term cash flow financing because we are not getting the cash in from sales. That is proving quite expensive because lenders now see us as a riskier investment and that means we are having to pay a higher interest rate. The market wants quarter-to-quarter growth and consistency of management and because we have not been providing that we are paying the penalty.'

Lucy saw he was not very happy about the situation, but she hadn't realized that Tom's prophesy about cash flow was going to come true quite so soon.

'What about our existing customers, are they paying on time?' This was something she needed to know after reading on the previous day on the internet that when customers started taking longer to pay their bills, it was a warning signal that you had an unhappy customer.

Simon again nodded in agreement. 'It is true, our Days Sales Outstanding, or the number of days our customers take on average to pay their bills has shot up from 45 to 90 days recently and for the first time ever we have even had to write off a number of bad debts.'

'Why do you think that's happening now as we haven't had a problem with it in the past?' Lucy was genuinely curious and wanted to know what Simon saw as the problem.

He ticked the items off on his fingers, and as he talked Lucy realized this could get embarrassing if he ran out of fingers. 'We are getting burnt at both ends: we are losing customers, so we have lost those recurring sales from them, we are not generating enough new sales and why the customers are taking longer to pay I think is because they are no longer happy with the product. For our customers to have any real faith in us the products have to speak for themselves but we are no longer as competitive as we were and our customers know it. New sales aren't coming in at the same rate as before, again because we don't have new, innovative products to offer, and the initial sales cycle is taking longer to close.

'Our products aren't as price-competitive as they were either and so all that makes it a much harder sell these days. That means even more delay at getting the money from the customer, and the amount of sales revenue is dropping anyway because we are selling less. I think you said you had already spoken to the sales department, so I am sure they will have told you that, in quite some detail! To make matters even worse, we have to discount more so our overall cost of each sale goes up and our profit per sale goes down.'

This was exactly what she had learned from the sales team but from the expression on Simon's face she could see that something more serious was to come. He leaned across the desk as if to emphasize the importance of what he was about to say. 'The fact is, Lucy, and I am sure you will treat this with the confidence it deserves, is that when Stephen joins as the new CEO, I am going to have to recommend to him straight away that we reduce our workforce. At the current levels of staffing and overheads, we will run out of cash within 12 months. We need to urgently implement a dramatic cost reduction programme and a priority is to get our staffing levels to an affordable level.'

From the quiet way he had spoken Simon was not trying to dramatize the situation but somehow she knew it was the truth. Without sales coming in from new customers, where was the cash going to come from? It was clear investors did not have confidence in Amroze Technology, even the bankers who would lend some short-term financing wanted a premium for lending to a higher risk company. It seemed Tom's philosophy of THEY BELIEVE extended to the bankers and investors, as well as the customers.

'Simon, you know that I'm working on this project for Stephen and what you have said is really valuable and will definitely help me with that. I appreciate how candid you have been. Is there anything else you think I ought to know?' Although, she wasn't sure if she would want to hear it, she knew she had to ask.

Simon thought for a second or two before replying. 'Well, it's more of the same really and part of the overall problem. We are not getting best value for money in many areas of the company, and although we have tried to tackle it there is still too much wastage and that leaches money, slowly but surely, and we cannot any longer turn a blind eye to it. We are going to have to cut costs right across the board, right down to the bone.'

This had not been the news Lucy had hoped to hear, but she could see it was the logical outcome of everything she had been told so far. Back in her office, she followed through on her decision of the previous evening to get Tom's support on where to go next and she called him at his office. At this stage she realized it wasn't going to come as a shock to Tom as it had so far played out exactly as he expected it to.

'Lucy, the situation you are facing at the moment is the inevitable consequence of poor sales; you are losing customers and without customers there is no revenue. If you think back to the days when you were a small start-up, what was it that Charlie used to say? "Customers and Cash" and he was absolutely right. Back then you were so close to the customers, and the cash they generated, that cash flow was always relevant because you knew that without cash you would not be paid. You could almost say to yourself "Great, Mr Jones has placed another order so that's my salary for the month taken care of!" These days, as you have got bigger, I suspect it is only people like Simon Ross who really think about cash at all.'

At the other end of the phone, Lucy smiled to herself as she did indeed remember thinking about one particularly large order they had got and how it meant she could plan her holiday that year without worrying whether or not she could afford it.

Tom expanded on this point as he knew it was critical for her to understand its importance if she was to make a credible plan to get the company moving again.

'The number one rule of entrepreneurial companies is not to run out of cash because without cash you are out of business. It is as simple as that. That principle does not just apply to small start-ups and cash-strapped entrepreneurs, it applies to large multinationals like yourselves. It even applies to industry giants like IBM who back in 1993 were literally months away from running out of cash. They had a turnover of multiple billions, but were losing money. In fact, their problem and yours are not dissimilar: their customers were no longer loyal and they just weren't buying computers like they used to. The world had moved on and in had come the PC, which left IBM with massive overheads and not enough sales to support it. As a company they had become complacent and had deluded themselves that they could survive whatever happened. In doing that they had lost sight of what really mattered – their customers.'

Lucy of course had heard the IBM story, as their fight back was a classic case study at business school, but a cash-flow problem of that scale was truly frightening. She waited to get more inside information from Tom and he didn't disappoint her.

'How they solved this situation was by going back to their entrepreneurial roots, back to the mindset that their founder Tom Watson had when he started the company. They chose to innovate and get close to their customers again. They brought their cash flow under control and yes, sadly had to resize, but in a crisis of that magnitude when you are against the wire you have to take drastic action. That's why Stephen is right to want a complete view of the company's problems as soon as he joins as CEO. He can't afford to wait, because the sooner you start to deal with the situation then the less harsh the solutions may have to be. The priority here must be to get your customers to believe in you again, then you will you be able to get the stock market to believe in you and then you will get the share price of the company back up again. The two go hand in hand.

'Now, the only way to get customers to believe again is to give them something to believe in. Lucy, I have said it now many times, and you have been hearing it on all sides with everyone you have spoken to. The real problem at Amroze is the products. They simply haven't kept pace with your customers' needs. Customers want innovative products and a service they can believe in that is consistently delivered. Amroze Technology's brand value will be destroyed if the customer is not happy, and trust me on this, once brand value is lost it is hard – and very expensive – to recover. It is only with clear innovation, new ideas, fresh thinking and creativity – all focused on the needs of your customers – that you will be able to turn things around.'

'Well I certainly can't disagree with that,' thought Lucy. 'The message has been totally consistent but what I need now are solutions!' Happily, Tom was going on to provide some ideas for her to start thinking about.

'Change is needed, and the first thing that must change is the mindset of the employees. They must now see themselves as entrepreneurial leaders who are driving change and innovation within the company. If what you are doing is not working (and it clearly isn't), then you must do something else. Only a fool keeps on doing the same thing expecting to get different results, and from what I know about Stephen Fox, he is nobody's fool. You must ask this question of yourself and others: "What would you do if this was your company? What would an entrepreneur do in this situation?" It is that type of thinking that will be the catalyst for turning your company around. Every thought should be about how we can make customers happy and how we can get new customers in. When your total focus is on the customer, then cash flow, share price, investor confidence – all those areas will no longer be a problem as they will all take care of themselves. If, however, you continue to focus on yourselves and your share price, then you will have taken you eye off the very thing that creates the value for you – your customers!'

Lucy finished writing her notes, and realized she had underlined customer three times, so she had certainly got the message. 'Thanks, Tom, that is really clear to me. Now I need to add this in to my work so far and then on to my next few meetings with the Human Resources people, and some of the employees.'

Tom sensed something in her voice so he wanted to reassure her that she was doing OK. 'Lucy, don't get disheartened. You are absolutely on the right track now, all you have to do is keep asking the right questions and together we will figure out what the answers mean!'

Feeling more confident, Lucy said goodbye and started thinking about what questions she could ask in her next few meetings.

TOM'S ADVICE

- It is not just customers who need to believe in your company, but shareholders, investors and analysts
- The number one rule of business is not to run out of cash — Think IBM (months away from running out of money in 1993)
- Profit is only one measure of success and can be manipulated, cash flow tells the truth about the success of your business
- Without positive cash flow from operations your business is going backwards
- Cash comes from happy customers who pay their bills on time. Without happy 'repeat' customers, your company will suffer
- Your share price is a function of belief and confidence. If investors and the market believe in your future growth prospects, your share price will rise; if they do not believe, your share price will fall
- Your company's ability to borrow at a competitive rate is a function of belief
- The value of your brand represents your customers' and the market's belief in your company.

Chapter Six

Lucy could not believe that it had been less than a week since she had had her first meeting with Tom, and how much she had managed to achieve in that short time. His threefold philosophy on belief seemed so simple, but she realized that it was giving her the blueprint to suggest a real way forward to use when she reported to Stephen later that month. After meeting and talking with so many of their customers she knew that Amroze had to return to a position where the customers got back their sense of belief in the company. She had consolidated Tom's wisdom of focusing on the customer and on innovation so that his core principle of THEY BELIEVE was the foundation of change in the company. With just two weeks to produce her report for Stephen she was beginning to think she might just get there, and with something worthwhile for him and for Amroze.

As she headed back to into the office on Monday morning she was ready to turn her attention to the next part of Tom's philosophy. He had been adamant that just convincing the customers that Amroze Technology had changed was only one of the steps that needed to be taken. What also had to change were the employees' attitudes and to get everyone in the company subscribing to WE BELIEVE. The idea of this, as Tom had explained, was to create belief and purpose within the team. In Amroze's case, that meant all of its 2000 employees, managers and executives. Although Lucy was not daunted by the size of the task she wasn't sure how easy it was going to be, and as she strode down the corridor to her office she had little idea how quickly it was going to become evident that belief and a unified sense of purpose within the entire organization did not exist.

The first thing Lucy always did was to check her diary to see if any of her appointments had been rearranged, but happily her first meeting of the week with Alexia Farr, head of human resources, was still pencilled in for midday. Alexia had not been able to meet with her until Monday lunchtime as, like Simon Ross in finance, she had had an urgent crisis meeting scheduled for the whole of that morning. Alexia had been apologetic to a degree, but had not been forthcoming about the details of the morning's meeting. From her initial reaction Lucy was conscious that this may be a tense meeting, particularly if Alexia was embroiled in difficult staffing issues at the moment. She arranged for them to go out to lunch together to try and create a more amiable environment.

Lucy had met Alexia on several occasions to talk over her own career progression at Amroze and had found her professional and very astute, but she knew that she could be quite reserved when put on the spot. Lucy had chosen a quiet restaurant not far from the office and, arriving first, settled herself at the table and got out her notebook to run through some of the questions she wanted to ask. She had about ten minutes before she saw Alexia coming across to the table. Taking a seat, she mumbled her apologies for the fact that her meeting had overrun. They exchanged some initial pleasantries but Lucy got the impression she was a little stressed.

'Alexia, I hope you don't mind if I write down the key points from our conversation?' Lucy asked, indicating her notebook.

'OK by me as long as you don't misquote me,' she responded half joking. Lucy realized she would need to tread carefully to get her to feel comfortable enough to speak openly.

'Well, at the very least I am getting to eat lunch today, which is something I didn't get too much time for last week! Seriously, I know it is going to be especially useful to get your particular take on the situation, so let's order and I will fill you in on what I am doing.' Eager to get started, they both quickly ordered. Once the waiter had left, Lucy launched into her now-familiar overview of her project and the report Stephen Fox had asked her to provide.

Alexia listened a little guardedly but when Lucy explained that she had recently had a detailed and informative meeting with the chief financial officer she seemed to visibly relax as if this was the green light she needed. When Lucy asked her for an overview of Amroze from an HR perspective she seemed happy to oblige. As she outlined the situation it sounded all too familiar to Lucy, but she hoped that there might be some good news buried in there somewhere.

'Well, Lucy, as you know, these are tough times for the company all round, and in HR we get the knock-on effect of that. When the company is not performing well, it is immediately reflected in employee morale. Frankly, at the moment it is at the lowest level that I can remember since I began working for Amroze over ten years ago. You don't need a business degree to see that there is a direct link between company performance and employee morale. When morale is high, our financial performance is high; when morale is low, our financial performance is even lower!'

Lucy thought back to her last conversation with Tom. It had been his suggestion that she meet with employees and HR this week and he had spoken at length to her about employee morale so what Alexia was saying came as no surprise. Tom had given her the example of a football match, where a team with low confidence and low morale had to compete against a team with high levels of confidence, drive and purpose. 'How can a football team expect to win matches if they do not believe or work together as a team?' Tom had asked her and of course she knew he was right. 'Well, a company has to act as a team as well. How can you expect the company to perform and achieve if they suffer from low morale and their employees are disillusioned?' After she had ended the call with him, she had tried to analyse just how far Amroze Technology was suffering from that particular problem and had set up the meeting with Alexia just afterwards. Lucy realized she had subconsciously been hoping that Alexia would be able to reassure her, but once again the picture was far from rosy. Realizing that Alexia was looking quizzically at her, she brought her attention back once more. 'Is profitability really such a key issue for HR? It seems a bit out of your area.' As soon as she said it, she realized it could be taken as a criticism and hoped that didn't sound as if she was suggesting Alexia was out of her depth.

'Absolutely key I am afraid and that's not just my opinion.' Luckily Alexia had taken the observation in the manner it was intended. 'There have been studies done that conclusively show that company morale is directly linked to profitability. It's a simple equation: low morale equals low profits and high morale equals high profits. It's obvious really, if you are happy with your job and your employer, you have more enthusiasm and energy for your work and that means you perform better.

From the company point of view we want happy employees, not least because it means we get much better rates of productivity and that naturally leads to greater profitability.'

Lucy had jotted down the key points and now needed to know if there were some more specific examples of what Alexia saw as the problems facing her directly as director of HR. Tom had asked her to get as much detail as possible so he could see how deep the company's problems were, and she suspected Alexia would be the one who could tell her but she knew she needed to choose her words carefully. 'That makes a lot of sense; are there any specifics you can think of that illustrate that for the purpose of the report?'

Alexia's eyes were reflective as she thought over what Lucy had asked. 'More specific, OK, let's see. Well, right now the share price is way down, so that means that most of the stock options our employees hold are worthless. Like most companies, stock options form a significant part of our compensation package and up to now many people stood to make a tidy amount of money from them as our share price was increasing. Unfortunately that is no longer the case; in reality, the price has been falling for some time and so their stock is worth far less. What I am hearing more regularly is people talking of leaving the company as they no longer have the financial incentive to keep them here and the other reasons that keep employees with a company just don't seem to be working either. When I talk to those who want to leave us, they don't seem to have a good reason to stay here any longer. When the stock options were worth something it helped keep our best talent; now, between you and me, I can perfectly understand their reasons for leaving.'

Lucy was intrigued by what those 'other reasons' to stay might be, but first she wanted to know more about those people who were leaving. 'Are you saying that staff turnover is abnormally high at the moment and that more staff are leaving than you would expect?'

'Yes, I'm afraid that is exactly what I am saying. We are losing many of our most talented people, though unfortunately not some of the ones we would be happy to see go. The best people have no trouble getting other good job offers; the "dead wood" that we seem to have more and more of just hang on as they know finding another job won't be easy. Of course, when your best people leave, it's the start of a downward spiral because that has an even bigger negative impact on the morale of those left behind. What we see in the remaining employees is an increase in behavioural problems; they take more sick days, are absent without notice, take longer lunch and coffee breaks and start arriving later and leaving earlier. All that means we have a severe drop in productivity and that has a real financial cost on the business. It is a difficult situation at the moment because once your staff stop believing in the company it can be very hard to get them motivated and we are about to make it worse for them.' At Lucy's enquiring look she shrugged and looked rather sad. 'It's also unfortunate, but right now we are in a situation where we are clearly going to have to cut staff to a level that can be supported by our reduced earnings. That was the conclusion we came to this morning, and once that news gets out it won't help morale either. Ideally we want to keep our best creative talent to help us out of this hole we are in, but as I said they are the ones who are first to leave. As they go to other companies it's common knowledge why they quit and then it becomes much harder to recruit fresh new creative talent. You know how the industry and the markets gossip, and at the moment everybody seems to know that Amroze Technology is having a hard time. Because we are not generating a profit we can no longer offer the big packages that would recruit the star players that we need.'

Lucy had been too busy to eat as she was taking notes and absorbing everything Alexia had told her. Amroze Technology was definitely on a downward spiral and right now it looked next to impossible to find a way out of the mess they seemed to be in. Determined to get at least some food that lunchtime, she dug her fork into her pasta as she reminded herself of one of Tom's comments about the growth cycles of companies who went from being a small entrepreneurial start-up to a full-blown corporate and the problems that could go with it. She twirled her fork around again as she sought for a possible reason for so many people leaving. 'You said that there were "other reasons" that kept people with a company, so it's not just that we are no longer able to offer competitive salaries and bonus packages?'

Alexia looked up from her plate and quickly shook her head. 'No, it's never just about money although that's often given as the reason. Believe me, Lucy, after many years in HR, I think I can confidently say that the main reason people leave is because they no longer believe in the company and don't feel appreciated for what they do. It's not the long-term goals that employees worry about; it's how they are treated every day. Lucy, you and I have been at Amroze almost from the beginning. If I think back to when we started with the company, when Charlie was in charge, we had a lot more fun then. Sure, we worked a lot harder, but none of us begrudged working long hours, because we all believed in what we were doing. It's much harder to do that when you have 2000 staff and a host of overseas offices.' She stopped, as if realizing that she had spoken with a real sense of loss.

'You know, it's a real cliché but people really are a company's best asset. Sometimes I have had a real struggle to make some of our past CEOs understand that. In fact, I would go further to say that sometimes our management structure actually demotivates employees and puts too much emphasis on responding to poor performance with criticism instead of giving praise when they do things well.' She sighed and shrugged her shoulders. 'Don't get me started on that particular hobby horse or we will be here all day!'

Lucy could see this was something Alexia was concerned about, so she definitely wanted to hear a bit more about it. 'Can you explain a little more about what you mean by the management structure getting in the way?'

Alexia looked a little hesitant. 'Look, Lucy, I'm very keen not to sound like I am criticizing Amroze, especially as I am part of the management team, but in the past few years we seem to have lost touch with our employees and have made it more difficult to find out how they are really feeling about the company. On a day-to-day basis we have more levels of management and that can hamper real communication. We seem to have a basic failure to communicate on all levels, and that's not helped by the fact there is now so much more paperwork and administration that people have to get involved in. They spend less and less time on doing the job we hired them for and what they enjoy doing. Again, one of the consequences of our poor profitability has been that we have had to cut the training budget and we know that training is something that employees appreciate. It shows we are investing in them, so when it stops they feel frustrated and start to wonder if they have a future with the company. Well, I guess that about says it all, and if I don't stop talking you are never going to get to finish your lunch!'

She smiled at Lucy as she said it, who took it as a signal that she would get no more insights that day and it was time to return to their food and move the conversation into more general areas so they could both relax a little. After lunch they returned to the office together, with Alexia off to yet another meeting to try to stem the continuing exodus of staff, and Lucy to write up her notes.

Lucy was beginning to look forward to her check-in sessions with Tom as it reinforced her feeling that she was not doing this all by herself but could call on his help when she needed it. Later that afternoon she rang him and related Alexia's points to him and he asked her to prioritize speaking first hand to as many current and past employees as she could manage. She agreed, and immediately rang Alexia to get contact details of those who had left and explained that she wanted to ask if they would tell her their reasons for doing so. She was happily surprised at how forthcoming Alexia was with the information and she was pleased that their meeting must have given Alexia some confidence in the process. Lucy spent the next couple of days setting up the appointments and over the next week she spoke with nearly 100 people, either in person or on the phone. What she had learned was very instructive. Particularly useful had been the dialogue with several small groups of people in the company itself, which had really brought the situation home to her. Again, Alexia had helped by circulating an email to employees asking those who were willing to meet with Lucy to come along to a series of meetings where they could air their views. The response had been encouraging, though the tone of the meetings had sometimes got a bit tense.

One in particular she remembered well, as it was held in the staff restaurant late in the day and there had been at least 50 people there. A cynical part of her thought they were attending because they got an hour off work in the middle of the afternoon but she was soon proven wrong. It just went to show how much employees actually appreciate being asked for their opinions. It had been the variety of people that had impressed her. They seemed to have come from most departments in the company and she knew she was getting the right information she needed to give to Stephen about what the employees felt was wrong with the company.

It was clear to Lucy that the employees really did know the company better than anybody else. She had been touched by the loyalty shown by some of those who had been with Amroze Technology for many years, and although times were now tough, not all of them were willing to write the company off just yet. She knew they needed to capitalize on this. What had really struck her was how eager some people were to make a contribution; they obviously felt sidelined and were glad of the opportunity to air their views. She remembered what Alexia had said about communication, and it was obvious no one had sought these people's opinions in a long time.

By the end of the week's meetings it was clear that no one was untouched by the current situation. They were all concerned and worried about their jobs and as Alexia had predicted, the rumour about mass redundancy was common knowledge and that made people even more nervous. Some were calculating their potential payouts, whereas many others were already looking for other jobs. There was a real feeling that they were on a sinking ship, but while some were ready to jump off, there were still those trying to hold on in the hope that things would change.

It now made sense to Lucy as to why their customers had complained so much about Amroze Technology in those first meetings she had had with them. If the employees were leaving in droves and those who remained were unmotivated and scared of losing their jobs, then it was no wonder the customers were getting passed from pillar to post and could not get answers to their problems. Put bluntly, many of their employees were now just turning up for the sake of their pay cheque and there was no sense of fun, passion or drive anywhere. The only thing some people were focused on was writing their resumes to apply for their next job and when they weren't doing that they were blaming the management, or their fellow workers for the company's problems. Sales blamed support, support blamed sales, marketing and finance blamed both internal and external factors but no one seemed willing to take real responsibility for their own part in the problem.

Lucy was again struck by the thought that one of the main themes from all her meetings was that people felt isolated. There was no communication either up or down within the company to highlight problems or celebrate any successes. There had been no sense of working towards a common goal, just lots of isolated individuals and departments getting on with their own work with no interaction on a regular basis with the others. No wonder things were going wrong and the more people focused on the problems the greater they seemed. Negativity had taken root in the company like a disease and it had spread to every single department.

She had reached the point in her notes where she had interviewed more recent employees and one particular meeting stood out in her mind. The meeting was with a young woman who had been at the company less than a year. Susan Armstrong worked in customer support where she was constantly bombarded with unhappy and irate phone calls from customers. She was only a young woman, but she was level headed and Lucy could see that her calm manner and reassuring tone of voice was a great asset in her job. She said frankly that she was very pleased to be asked for her views, as she had kept trying to pass on comments before but felt she was never getting anywhere. Susan had clearly never known the good times at Amroze, as she had joined when the company was already in decline. As Lucy knew only too well, customer support was the real sharp end and she had heard the customers' side of the story; how they never got phoned back or had their problems sorted out and now she heard it from the company perspective. Susan was clearly a conscientious person and very unhappy about the way Amroze was being run. She was under constant pressure from dissatisfied customers and when she managed to pass them on to the right department with their complaint they often came straight back to her saying that not only had they not got a satisfactory answer, but that the person they had spoken to either couldn't care less or had actually been rude to them. It was vital that their concerns got fed back to management, and Susan tried to do that but felt she was not taken seriously. It seemed to her that management were too busy with other issues to take notice of what really mattered, and for her that was the customers.

Sensing Susan was a willing and informed candidate, Lucy had asked her what she felt the real problem was. Susan's eyes had lit up and she had been very passionate and critical about the communication within the company. She was tired of having to fob customers off and tired of being accused by them of never passing on their complaints, which she vehemently told Lucy she did. In fact, she brought with her a file containing copies of customer complaints and as Lucy looked through she saw that Susan had dated and noted each one with details of who it had been passed to and on a separate top sheet she listed what date they got back to her and what action was taken. She reminded Lucy of herself when she was starting out and hoped Amroze didn't lose her, although the sad reality was this was exactly the kind of employee that would be knocking on the doors of their competitors looking for something to believe in.

It was clear that the majority of Susan's notes consisted of 'contacted department head on the 3rd, no response.' And that same message was repeated with a number of different dates sometimes up to a dozen times over a period of a week. She confirmed that she always kept a log and that the response to her messages was mainly indifference and a 'we will get round to it, stop fussing' message that she found both patronizing and very frustrating. She had felt just as bad when she had made suggestions to improve the system for both the staff and customers and no one in management seemed to be the slightest bit interested. Susan made it very clear that for her this was a major problem within Amroze and although others Lucy had met that week had spoken about the poor communication within the company, she made the point more forcefully and persuasively than the others had.

Time to leave the office; after an exhausting week of non-stop meetings, Lucy was more than glad to have a face-to-face meeting with Tom at a coffee shop close to his office.

In the two weeks since Tom had first met her, Lucy had taken on board quite a few new ideas, and the tight deadline and the endless meetings had definitely taken their toll. Tom could see the strain on her face and yet he thought she seemed enthusiastic, as if she could see the end in sight. She confirmed that by exclaiming 'One week to go!' as she sat down opposite him and toasted him with the coffee he had ordered for her. 'Glad to see you are in good spirits,' he remarked as she settled herself down and got out her notebook. He listened as usual in silence until she had gone through her findings from the interviews she had done that week. When she had finished Tom sat back and thought for a moment about what she had discovered.

'Lucy, before you started the week, I explained briefly to you the concept of WE BELIEVE and what you have found this week has shown you just what happens when that is no longer the case. Just like with THEY BELIEVE, where the customer must believe in you, with WE BELIEVE it is the employees and the management team who must believe in the company. From everything you have told me, it will be obvious to you that, in the majority of cases, this belief has been lost.' Lucy nodded her head in agreement, a little deflated by what he had said, so Tom turned his attention to showing her how things could be turned around.

'You know my view by now that belief is everything. How can anything be achieved by someone who does not 100% believe in what they are doing? The fact that your staff turnover is high and that existing staff are polishing their resumes ready to quit tells me loud and clear that they have doubts about Amroze Technology, and they no longer believe in it. No company can ever expect to succeed without a 100% motivated, focused and driven team working towards a unified common goal. The team must live and breathe the message of WE BELIEVE, but that only works if they have something to believe in. At the moment, just like the customers, it seems the staff have very little to give them confidence.'

Lucy had been listening intently and as he paused she agreed with him, 'I know that's true because just about everywhere I went in the company it seemed that everyone had given up hope, they were almost waiting for the axe to fall. How can we possibly turn that amount of negativity around?'

Tom was watching her thoughtfully and Lucy realized he had the answer and had been waiting for her to ask the right question.

'The first thing you do is stop thinking like an employee and start thinking like an entrepreneur and ask yourself, "What would I do if this was my company?" You know, when I met my business mentor, Michael Redford, he gave me a formula to create belief. He made it simple by making each letter of BELIEVE stand for something. Let me give you this formula and explain how this philosophy will help turn things around for you.'

Lucy flipped over to a new page in the notebook and got ready to hear what Tom had to say.

'Firstly, the "B" of BELIEVE. This stands for "**Be Passionate and Want it**". Your team needs to be passionately in love with what they do. Look at any successful individual or team – the common bond between them is that they love what they are doing and they have a burning desire to achieve it. They are almost obsessed with what they are doing. I suspect when Charlie was there, the whole team had this burning desire and obsession to create a great company. From what I know of Charlie, I also suspect the desire was for happy long-term repeat customers and generating cash. It seems to me that there is no passion or obsession now.' Lucy remembered what Alexia had said about how there was no fun at work any more and how she had missed the old days with Charlie and being part of a team. Was that what Tom was getting at?

Oblivious to her thoughts, Tom continued with his explanation. 'The "E" of BELIEVE stands for "**Extend Your Comfort Zone**". How many people in your company are really stretching themselves and doing something that makes them uncomfortable rather than just coasting along? We identified right at the beginning that complacency was the real killer within Amroze Technology and if you study business at all – as I know you have – then you will see that great companies and great teams constantly stretch and challenge themselves. They tackle their fears and limiting beliefs head on, in just the same way that great sports teams and high achievers do. It is the only way to succeed. It strikes me that Amroze Technology no longer does this, but I bet my bottom dollar that they did when they were a small start-up company. How else could they have grown so fast?

'Next comes "L" for "**Lies and Luck Don't Work**". This is one I believe Amroze Technology have certainly been guilty of. Lying to themselves that they know what the customer wants, being complacent, waiting for luck to create opportunity rather than getting out there, innovating, getting close to customers, to their market and creating their own luck. Just imagine if all 2000 staff at Amroze Technology really understood what was going on in your industry, with the market and your competitors. Imagine if you had the communication lines in place to harness that knowledge. Imagine if all 2000 staff really understood what your customers wanted, how changes in their industry, their customers and their markets had changed their needs; and imagine if you as a company were able to tap into that knowledge and create innovative products and services to meet the needs of your customers. You would be unstoppable, but instead, you rely on luck.'

This concept of luck and lies was entirely new to Lucy, but she was certainly intrigued by the idea and could see the logic in what Tom was saying.

'Now for the real key to creating success in your company. This is the "I" of BELIEVE. "I" stands for "**Install Goals**". It seems to me that what is missing at Amroze Technology is a common goal that everybody believes in. We will speak more about this next time we meet, but I believe this will be the key recommendation you need to make to Stephen when you write your report. For now, just realize that without a common purpose that everybody believes in, is passionate about and has a burning desire to achieve, how can you realistically expect to outperform your competitors? Let me tell you plainly, that the only real purpose you can have as a company is to satisfy your customers. Without customers you do not have a company and it strikes me that Amroze Technology is doing a great job of losing customers and running out of cash. You could say it's almost their only growth area!'

'That's definitely not the kind of growth that we should be encouraging!' was Lucy's quick retort as Tom paused and took a breath.

'Not at all! Now, the next "E" stands for "**Enjoy Hard Work**". When Charlie was there, you have told me that the team did work hard but had fun at the same time. The fun angle is very important; if you don't enjoy doing what you do, you will not put the same level of effort into it. This company was fun to work in once, and it can be fun to work in again – but you must be able to make it fun for the team. Only then will the team be willing to make the sacrifices it takes to become a great company again. Only when you have a clear purpose to work towards will the team have the self-discipline to tackle the necessary hard and probably unpleasant tasks that will have to be done to turn the company around.'

Tom paused to check that Lucy was keeping up with him and she used it as an opportunity to show she was following. 'I have heard from so many people how they used to enjoy working for Amroze, it would be great to get that spirit back again. Not sure about the "hard and unpleasant tasks" bit though.'

Tom wasn't about to let her off the hook on this point. 'You know, you don't get one without the other, not at the stage Amroze is at. That leads me nicely on to the last two parts of I BELIEVE, the "V" and "E". The "V" stands for "**Very, Very Persistent**". The team must realize that no matter how much effort they put in, the success of the company is not guaranteed. I suspect after the tough times you have been going through recently they will understand that clearly. But what they may not know is that great teams succeed by never giving up on achieving their common purpose. If a team believes passionately in what they are trying to achieve, if they have a clear purpose which everybody believes in and identifies with – then why would they give up or accept no for an answer? If you want to help make Amroze Technology a great company again, and you want to learn from entrepreneurs and reignite the entrepreneurial spirit in Amroze, then getting the team to have total tenacity is fundamental. You need an iron-willed team who know what they want to achieve and will make it happen at all costs. Look at the experience of the Americans when they decided to put a man on the moon. At that time it was a crazy idea, there was not the knowledge or technical expertise, just a passionate belief that it could be done. It took many years and constant failure, but they persevered, they kept going. They got a man on the moon but they wouldn't have done it if they had given up every time things went wrong. And that leads me to the final "E", which that example also fits.'

Lucy had been too young to see the first moon landing, but she knew from her own experience the importance of never giving up. Whatever she had wanted in her life she had followed it with a dogged persistence, whatever the setbacks, and she could see exactly what Tom was getting at.

This "E" stands for "**Expect Failure**". The team must realize that you can not achieve success without failure. The two go hand-in-hand, but it is how you deal with failure that counts. You could argue that Amroze Technology is going through a period of failure right now, but at the same time it is creating great opportunity for change. Good things can come from this and this is a clear opportunity to turn the fortunes of the company around. You must, as you are doing, learn from your failure as a company and use that knowledge to change your actions. If you do nothing, then you really will fail.'

Lucy felt the seriousness of the situation as Tom outlined it, and gratefully she realized he wanted her to have all the tools at her disposal to start turning the company around. Tom saw she had finished her coffee and waved across to the waiter to bring them some refills. 'I need you to stay really awake so I can be sure you have understood what I am telling you!' he joked and she smiled back at him. 'Lucy, these principles of BELIEVE can be applied to either a team – which I want you to remember as WE BELIEVE – or an individual – which I want you to remember as I BELIEVE. Either way, the more of the principles you apply to the team, or the individuals within the team, the greater the success of the company will be. But, let me tell you now – for all of this to work, the company needs to have a common purpose. It seems to me it is lacking this and therefore without the "I" of "Install Goals" in place, the system will not work. Only when you have that clear sense of purpose, can you see a real and tangible outcome that can unite all 2000 members of staff. It's only then that the turnaround will start to happen. I'll drink to that.' He raised his coffee cup and toasted her with it.

'Thanks,' she responded, 'not much for me to do there then!' as she raised her cup to his in mock salute.

TOM'S ADVICE

- Employees must believe in the company and its products and services (WE BELIEVE)
- There is no room for doubt in the minds of employees. If employees do not believe, how can they make customers believe?
- Morale and profitability are linked. High morale = high profitability. Low morale = low profitability
- Companies need to attract 'talent'. It is passionate, talented people who create successful products and services which customers can believe in
- Communication is critical to create high levels of morale and belief within the company
- Employees must make decisions as if the company was their own. When faced with a difficult situation, they must ask themselves 'What would an entrepreneur do in this situation, or what would I do if this was my company?'

Chapter Seven

When Tom had run through his description of BELIEVE it had struck a real chord with Lucy. Now, as she sat in her office the following morning she saw that when she looked back through her notes, it had been the subconscious pattern emerging from practically everything she had written. Whether she looked at the notes she had taken from her interviews with staff or with customers, she could see words jumping off the pages which spelt out exactly what Tom had been talking about. There was a real loss of belief both inside and outside the company.

This was her last chance to get more information as she had to submit her report to Stephen by the following week and so she had set up a meeting for later in the day with Emma Macintyre and Jon Patel in consulting. They were not newcomers to the company: Emma had worked at Amroze for seven years and Jon for four years, so Lucy knew they had plenty of experience working with clients and knew the products inside out. 'I hope they can give me some more insight into what they think the problems are,' was her thought as she went into the meeting, and she was certainly not disappointed.

Lucy was aware that they were probably regularly dealing with angry customers and was prepared for some defensiveness on their part. However, they were pleased to be asked and, after some initial suspicion, were reassured by Lucy's carefully chosen words regarding confidentiality.

It was no surprise that their comments echoed much of what she had heard during the week and were definitely sending the same message. They had both heard about Lucy's visits to the other parts of the company and knew why she wanted to talk to them so Lucy's opening explanation was kept brief. Emma looked at Jon and a silent agreement passed between them that she should go first and outline for Lucy what their situation was. She was a young woman in her late twenties who gave the impression of someone who was dependable, and knew what she was talking about. 'I bet she inspires confidence in the customers,' reflected Lucy as Emma explained clearly and concisely what procedures were in place in the consulting department when the project is handed over from the sales team. 'Without these kinds of people on board we would probably have gone under already,' thought Lucy and made a note of just that to include in her report.

'We go in to the customer after the sales team, and if we are lucky, we get a sales handover report from them. That should outline the project, the budget, what the business problems are and what the customer's expectation is.' That emphasis on the word 'should' wasn't lost on Lucy so she wasn't too surprised when Emma went on to give her more of the true picture.

'Now it is not an exaggeration to say that nine times out of ten, most of this information is incomplete or inaccurate. Sometimes it is also very clear to us that the budget to complete the project is inadequate.' She glanced at Jon who smiled his agreement as she continued. 'Managing the customer's expectation is our biggest challenge. After the sales team have finished their sales pitch, the customer's expectation is right up here,' Emma raised her right hand to the level of her ear to make her point. 'However, the problem is that the budget we have to implement the system with brings the reality of what we can achieve down here.' She lowered her hand to waist level. 'Now somehow, we need to try to close that gap, but frankly it is near impossible. The biggest problem is that the software simply does not work in the way the sales team suggest that it does.' By now Emma was looking frustrated and had obviously been wanting for some time to get this message across to someone who would listen. 'I know they need to present a positive spin to sell our software, and that it is a hard sell these days, but if it does not do what they suggest it can, then we cannot deliver the impossible.'

All the time Emma had been speaking Jon was nodding his head in agreement. He was younger than Emma, and Lucy thought he looked a little irritated and edgy, as if he was at the end of his patience with Amroze and had had enough of not being able to do a good job. As Emma finished speaking he looked sympathetically at her and on her cue he took up the story from her.

'Everything Emma has said is true and, after a while, it starts to get to you on a personal level as well. We obviously want to give our clients the best service and best products, but when every client is dissatisfied and we know before we even start that we will not be able to meet their expectations, it is bound to affect you. You find yourself not wanting to talk to clients because you can't bear to let them down and admit that you can't deliver what they are expecting. How do you think that makes us feel?'

Lucy acknowledged that he had a good point, and she could easily imagine just how frustrated and unhappy it would make her in that situation. Maybe it was time to ask a really tough question. 'Do you think clients are better off as a result of buying Amroze's technology?' Emma didn't need any time to think about it, her response was immediate.

'Not always, no, and that is the problem in a nutshell. I don't want to stand in the way of any sales because we all know how we desperately need all the sales we can get just to survive at the moment. But the sales we are getting are simply not realistic in terms of what we can deliver and so we are bound to have unhappy customers. Sadly, I am afraid Jon is absolutely right. Sometimes we don't want to speak with customers when we have to admit that they have been sold a promise that we cannot live up to.'

This was getting more controversial, but Stephen had said he wanted to have the fullest picture possible, and Lucy had the strongest feeling that this was really getting to the heart of the problem. She asked Jon the same question and he emphatically agreed with Emma.

'I don't like saying it, but no, I'd go further than Emma and say I definitely do not think our customers are better off buying Amroze technology. I know for a fact that a number of them would be much better off with our competitors' products. I am right aren't I, Emma?' Lucy looked over at her and Emma nodded to confirm that what he had said had her full agreement before turning again to speak to Lucy.

'When I first started here, I would have said yes, without question, our customers were better off with our products, but not now. What our customers want, and how much they want to pay has changed radically over the past few years. I know our competitors have invested heavily in their new products and they meet customer needs at a lower price than ours. Lucy, this is not just Jon and me moaning. We are certainly not the only people who think like this. I speak with many of our consulting teams around the world and they all face the same issues with customers. We are all at our wits' end with having to deal with this incredibly frustrating situation day in and day out. There just doesn't seem to be an end in sight.'

Lucy could hear Tom's words about belief echoing in her mind. He had said many times that what was needed was not just THEY BELIEVE from their customers but it was also vital that WE BELIEVE had to come from the employees. Lucy glanced at Emma and Jon, and it was obvious that they were both sincere in what they had said, and she was sure they were pretty representative of the very staff who were responsible for implementing Amroze Technology's products. It was clear they did not believe in either the products or the company so, again, it was no wonder that the customers didn't believe either. Lucy fleetingly thought that she could just draw a line under the conversation right then and there, but she wanted to be thorough so she pressed them both for more details about the everyday occurrences that had contributed to this lack of belief.

It made dismal hearing. There were too many tales of recent problems where implementation had gone wrong and customers were refusing to pay their bills and demanding to see the person who sold them the technology in the first place. She had made plenty of notes so she closed the meeting and thanked them for their time. As they left her office she pulled out her diary to check her next appointment and realized she only had a couple of minutes before she was due in customer support. Closing the door behind her, she headed down the corridor and reminded herself of the conversation with Susan Armstrong who was also in the same department. That conversation had given her a fairly clear idea of what to expect from this next meeting with Dominic Kerris and she imagined it was going to bring up some of the same major issues. Dominic was in the front line for seeing the stark reality of Amroze Technology's customer relations as he was one of a team of 25 people responsible for taking phone calls when they had problems with their technology. She had agreed to meet with him in the small coffee area next to the open-plan support office and watched for a few moments through the glass window that divided the area off. She was immediately struck by how few people were manning the phones and she had to wait for Dominic to finish a call before he could come over and speak with her. He immediately apologized and said he would only be able to have a very brief meeting because there were only four staff in the office today. Out of a pool of 25 people there would normally be ten at any one time, but as he made clear to her, support suffered probably the lowest morale in the company. He seemed quite resigned to the fact that they had very high absenteeism and took as a matter of regular occurrence the fact that just yesterday two members of the department had handed in their notice. One man had gone off with long-term stress-related illness and one of their longest-serving women employees was taking a well earned, and overdue, vacation.

'Well, Susan did warn me that things were bad here, but this looks like a department whose morale is at rock bottom.'

Lucy pushed that thought aside and put a friendly smile on her face. She didn't want to put any more pressure on Dominic because it was obvious from what he was telling her that the strain of talking to angry and dissatisfied customers all day had taken a heavy toll on the people who worked there. Dominic was perfectly polite, but he seemed tired and apathetic. All the time they spoke his eyes kept turning to look over at a large digital screen in the centre of the floor of the support area. This showed the number of customers waiting on the phone, and the number of open support issues that had not yet been resolved. As they briefly talked Lucy could see that the number of calls waiting was growing and the list of outstanding issues was getting bigger too. She didn't want to keep him too long, as he was clearly worried about the growing numbers on the board, so she asked him to briefly outline what he believed were the main problems for his department.

Dominic pulled his glance back from the board, and seemed unsure where to start. Lucy looked encouragingly at him, so he cleared his throat and his soft voice came a little hesitatingly. 'What do I believe are the main problems?' He attempted a smile. 'How long have you got?! Actually, I'm not sure what to think anymore. I used to believe we had a good company and great products, but to be honest I lost that faith a long time ago. Working in customer support can do that to you because you just get continually ground down. Every day more customers are on the phone saying they have a problem; for instance, that a particular function of the product is not working.

'Now, of course we know what the most common problems are and some of those we can fix over the phone, but there are quite a few that we just cannot fix at all. In fact, the number that we cannot fix is growing daily and it is those ones we have to pass onto product development because they need to build the fix into the main product. This doesn't solve the problem for the customer in the short term because it means they have to use a work-around before they get a new version of the product with the fixes in it. This does not impress them and why should it? They have spent so much money on this technology, which we have told them will make their company more efficient and then they have to use these manual work-arounds, so it is no wonder they are not happy. And, between you and me, some issues never even get a fix at all and the customer needs to work-around for ever.' He glanced at the board again and the number of waiting calls made him rise to his feet. 'I'm sorry, Lucy, but I really must get back. The number of customers trying to get through is growing and I need to take some of these calls. You are welcome to stay and listen, and before you leave take a look at the board. Check how long our list of unresolved issues is. Unfortunately that list is growing daily.' He went back into the support area and picked up a headset to take a call.

Lucy followed him out and was glad he had given her the opportunity to stay around and hear exactly what the situation was. For the next hour she heard a constant refrain of apology and excuses from the four support team members to the callers and it was obvious that some customers were very angry indeed. More than once she saw one of the operators wince and hold the headset away from their ears and she marvelled that they managed to stay as polite as they did, though there was no enthusiasm or energy in their voices, it was as if they were just going through the motions.

As she stood looking through the list of outstanding issues on the board she saw that each one was assigned a level of urgency and a date when it was first reported. Some with a lower level of urgency had never been fixed, just as Dominic had said, even though the problem required an extensive manual work-around. Lucy could imagine the customer wasting time doing manual processes each month as a way of making up for the deficiency in the system and their temper and frustration levels rising as a result. She thought back to the expectation gap Emma in consulting had referred to and wondered if the issues on the support list had anything to do with them. She wrote down the specifics of the product complaints in her notebook and marked with an asterisk those that had been on the board for over a month with no resolution.

As she left the area she glanced over at Dominic to say goodbye but he was heavily involved in a call that had him running his hands wearily through his hair so she thought it was best to just leave him to it. Lucy knew she needed to get her report finished by the end of the week and because she had spent less time in support than she had allocated due to the pressure they were under, she now had some free time before her next meeting with the head of product development. She went back to her office and sat down at her desk where there were a couple of phone messages waiting for her. She listened quickly and decided they could wait until later as she took out her notebook and spent the next hour or so thinking through the outline of her report for Stephen and trying to see where there were gaps in her knowledge that she still needed to fill before she could begin it. She became totally absorbed and was startled when her organizer beeped to warn her that her next meeting was due in five minutes' time. She grabbed her notebook and headed up the three floors to product development, reflecting that at least Stephen's project was helping her keep fit!

As she pushed open the doors to the team area she felt a fond rush of nostalgia. The office and the people looked exactly how she remembered them from her previous time of working at HQ. They were casually dressed in jeans and t-shirts, with cups of coffee and bottles of water covering practically every surface. It was hard to see the surface of the desks as they were cluttered with manuals, papers and Post-It notes stuck round the sides of the monitors. Lucy had a momentary flashback to the incredibly neat office of Simon Ross, the CFO, and thought he would probably have a heart attack if he had to work in this chaos. But as she well knew, this was an area where nonconformity was not just tolerated, but actually encouraged, as people needed to have a more creative outlook for the problem solving they had to do. As she glanced around, Lucy was again struck by how few people were there. The company had got significantly bigger, and yet this department had fewer people in it than when she was last there. It puzzled her so she mentally added it to the list of questions she had planned to ask.

J.P. Wiseman, head of product development, was very welcoming but as he had only been in the post for a couple of months Lucy wasn't sure just how much input he would be able to give her. She had heard from customers and employees as to where the problems in the company lay, and it seemed to Lucy that at the heart of everything was the product. If the product worked and the customers loved it, as was the case when Charlie was there, then all was well. If the product did not work then naturally the customers did not love it, and the inevitable downward slide everywhere in the company was a direct consequence of that.

'Call me J.P.,' had been the casual greeting Lucy had received as she was greeted by a man only slightly older than she was. His blond curly hair was long, though neatly cut and he was as casually dressed as his staff. His office had a pair of oars mounted on the wall and his sweatshirt bore the logo of his old college that Lucy knew had a great reputation for producing fine rowers. She had to admit he was not quite what she had expected. He saw her glance at the oars and his mouth twitched upwards so he was probably used to that kind of reaction. He was very quick to appreciate what she wanted from the meeting with him and had obviously done his homework in his short time with the company. J.P. knew exactly what was wrong with his department and surprisingly offered no excuses. He was the first to agree that the product was not up to scratch.

'We have to be honest and face facts. Once Amroze Technology was the leading technology in the market place but now we have seriously fallen behind our competitors. We took our eye off the ball and no one seemed to be really aware that our customers' needs and requirements had changed and moved on. Unfortunately, from what I can see in even my short time here, the company failed to invest in its products. They seemed to think that because they had been market leaders they could afford to rest on the success they had in the early days. Without that investment my hands are tied. The reality is that customers wanted innovation and new products and Amroze allowed its competitors to take that market from them.'

Lucy thought this might be the right time to ask him why there were so few people in the office. J.P. shrugged. 'All the really innovative people got tired of not having any quality investment in the department. It looks to me as if it was just left to drift. Good people like to have challenges; they are here because they like producing new ideas and seeing them developed. When that isn't happening they tend to get disillusioned and then start looking for other jobs. I think the department is about 25% down on what it was a few years ago and there hasn't been any investment in recruiting new, top people.' He offered her a quick smile. 'Apart from me, of course!'

Lucy couldn't help smiling back although she wondered if he was doing anything to address this and she needed some more answers. As if he read her thoughts he turned to the open door of his office and called through to his assistant to bring him the document he had just printed off. 'It is critical that we get closer to the market and find out exactly what our competitors are doing.' He handed Lucy the document his assistant had given him. 'This is just the first draft of a competitor analysis report. It needs some work, but this will give you a fairly good idea of what we are up against.' Lucy took the bulky document from him, and from the sheer weight of pages could see that he had already put a lot of time and investigation into it but she wasn't sure she had enough time to go right through it before her deadline. 'This is an impressive amount of data, but can you give me an overview?'

'If you want the quick summary, then what I have found is that our biggest threat is not from the people who we thought were our traditional competitors. The real danger now comes from a new, small start-up company who have developed their solution using the latest internet-based software. This costs a fraction to develop and deploy compared to what our costs are and I think we have got to learn from their example.'

This was certainly news to Lucy who imagined he was going to name several of their leading competitors. 'What's the name of the company?'

'C.G. Enterprises. They are a great, innovative, exciting company with a terrific team and one that I believe we should be trying to emulate. It was set up a year ago by a guy called Charlie Gardham. I think he was the entrepreneur who started Amroze Technology originally, wasn't he?'

Lucy felt her mouth drop open. That piece of information left her in no doubt whatsoever, that getting back that original spirit of when Charlie was at Amroze was critical to their future success and smiled to herself at the irony of it all. 'He was the original founder, yes. I had no idea that Charlie had gone on to start another company. We all thought when he sold Amroze he didn't want to run a company ever again. Well, if anyone would know how to beat us in the marketplace it would be him! So what do you think is the answer to the situation?'

J.P. shrugged and pointed to the report he had given her. 'It's all in there. I think there can only be one answer, and that is to make our products better. We need to understand exactly what our customers want and we need to give it to them at the right price. If we can't do that, we may as well all go home right now, because if we carry on as we are Amroze Technology will not be in business 12 months from now.'

J.P.'s relaxed manner did not conceal the fact that he was seriously worried. Although he had been in the company for a very short period, Lucy could see that he had a clear idea of what was needed and just like Charlie, he understood the importance of giving the customers what they wanted. She left him to get on with finalizing his report and went back to put her notes in order before calling Tom later that evening.

Lucy's phone call to her mentor was destined to be a short one, but as usual there were nuggets of wisdom to be gleaned from it. She opened the conversation with a fairly confident statement. 'You made the point a long time ago and now everything is pointing towards it. If we do not offer our clients the best products at the best price and products that meet their needs, then of course we will lose out to our competitors.'

'Great, I am glad you can see it so clearly.' Tom had been waiting for Lucy to identify the real problem with Amroze Technology and he sounded genuinely pleased with her. 'The market you're in is so competitive and customers have so much choice, there is a real battle to secure the belief I keep talking about. You may have the best marketing in the world, but if your products or services do not back that up, then sooner or later you will be caught out. What every company needs is constant and never-ending innovation, always focusing on the needs of the customer. This is how you will start to turn around the fortunes of Amroze Technology.'

Innovation had been something that J.P. Wiseman had talked about too, thought Lucy when Tom went off on another abrupt change of subject.

'Tell me, do you have an iPod, Lucy?' Glad of some light relief she smiled and responded that she did.

'Yes, you and just about every other person of your generation. Why do I want to know? Because the iPod is the perfect example of a product that turned a company's fortunes around and re-ignited their entrepreneurial spirit. Some years back, Apple computers was drifting and had lost much of its market share to the PC. Steve Jobs, who was one of the original founders of Apple, actually came back to the company after some years away. Initially he was their iCEO, and before you ask it stands for interim CEO, but I always thought it was a cool title anyway! Under Steve's direction, Apple recreated the belief and passion that was originally in the company when he first started it. They looked at how the world was changing, how their customers lived their lives and how new technology was changing peoples lives. Out of that, they developed the iPod, which I think you will agree completely resurrected Apple's fortunes. They didn't sit still and continue selling their existing products to an ever-shrinking market. They innovated and applied the principles of constant and never-ending innovation. Apple never stands still, because the world doesn't stand still. The needs of their customers are constantly changing and they keep changing to meet that.

They rekindled the passion for their products and when you look at what they have produced it is clear those products have been designed with love. They are so beautiful, and the team that worked on them must be so proud of them. The customers love them too and now the word iPod has become a household name, like Hoover and Google. As I mentioned to you in one of our previous conversations, when that happens you know you have something that your customers really believe in. What Amroze Technology needs to do now is follow Apple's great example, and I'm glad to hear that the new head of development is getting a handle on this. You must start to create new innovative products that your customers and your employees can believe in. Only when you are applying and living the principles of THEY BELIEVE and WE BELIEVE will success come, as it has at Apple.'

Lucy was once again scribbling notes and she thought Tom had finished, but he had one more thing he wanted to say to her.

'You have done some great work, but there is one more subject we need to look at before you write that report. Remember that my belief system has three parts: we have talked about THEY BELIEVE and WE BELIEVE and now we need to look at I BELIEVE. This is perhaps the key element for you to get across to Stephen: the subject of leadership. I'd like to meet you in person to talk about this rather than on the phone, so can you meet me tomorrow in our regular coffee shop at around five in the afternoon?'

Lucy hastily agreed, and couldn't wait to hear what this final piece of the puzzle might be. At last she was getting near to writing that final recommendation.

TOM'S ADVICE

- Great marketing can only take a company so far, sooner or later the products and services must stand up to scrutiny
- Only outstanding products and services at the right price will ultimately outsell competitors
- Competition can come out of the blue from new start-ups as well as traditional sources
- Only by understanding the detailed needs of your customers can you build great products and services for them
- Constant and never-ending innovation and product development is essential for long-term growth and to avoid complacency and decline (Think iPod)
- It is employees who create great products and services for customers. Employees must therefore first say 'WE BELIEVE'.

Chapter Eight

Lucy arrived a few minutes early at the coffee shop and felt she was too buzzed for any caffeine so she ordered a peppermint tea and as she waited for Tom, she thought about his specific request that they have this meeting in person. He obviously felt this was important, and since she knew that he wanted to talk to her about the third element of reigniting the entrepreneurial spirit within a company, she couldn't help being excited about what he would have to say. Having spent the last few weeks exploring what the problems were with the company, the employees and the product, she wasn't sure how much more there was to say but she had confidence that if Tom thought it was important, then it surely would be. All she knew was that it was all about the principle of I BELIEVE, which from previous things Tom had said she understood to be about leadership.

The waiter was bringing her tea over when she saw that Tom was walking into the café. He ordered a double espresso before settling down and saying hello.

'That's a good shot of caffeine, are you afraid you might doze off?'

'I always need my wits about me with you, Lucy,' Tom commented. 'You don't miss a trick, which is, I suspect, exactly why Stephen Fox gave you this job! So let's get down to the reason why I wanted to see you face to face. I know you have done great work with all the interviews you have done and your analysis of what is wrong with the company is right on target. However, there is still one key element that has to be addressed and that is leadership.'

Lucy's notebook was now so much a part of her she hardly noticed that she had it open and ready on the table. She didn't want to interrupt Tom with too many questions; what she was really focusing her attention on was on writing down these final key points.

He saw her notebook and smiled as he took a couple of mouthfuls of coffee and settled back in his chair as he organized his thoughts for her.

'Lucy, you now know that in order for a company to be successful the two principles of THEY BELIEVE and WE BELIEVE have to be operating freely and fully. The key to creating that situation is understanding that it can only be brought about by strong leadership. In other words that third element I talked to you about has to be present or the rest will fail. That element is I BELIEVE. It is leaders who inspire teams – and it is teams who create great products and services that customers can believe in. Without strong leadership, at all levels, the rest of the business will suffer.'

Lucy glanced up from her notes, as she heard something in Tom's voice that she hadn't noticed before. He is really passionate about this, she thought as she forgot her resolve and asked him a question. 'At all levels? You mean right down to the shop floor?'

Tom nodded emphatically. 'Yes, you may typically think that it is the role of the CEO to be the leader of the company, but in reality, great companies have great leaders at all levels. I would go as far as to say that in great companies, each and every employee sees themselves as a leader, an enterprise leader. That doesn't mean a case of too many chiefs and not enough Indians. It means that each employee must own the change and feel responsible for innovation in line with customer and market demands, whatever their part in it is.'

That was a phrase that made Lucy look enquiringly at him. 'I know we talked about entrepreneurial leaders some time ago but I haven't heard of an enterprise leader before.'

'You may not have heard of it, but you need to understand it if Amroze Technology is going to be turned around. I believe that great companies create great enterprise leaders. These are companies that really understand and connect with their customers, create passion and belief within their team and have a strong purpose that everybody resonates with. You can easily recognize enterprise leaders because they are people who understand that their role within the company is to help it achieve its overall purpose. They are people who follow the BELIEVE philosophy that I have outlined to you. Let's just recap it.' He used his fingers to tick off each letter as he worked his way through them.

'B – They are prepared to "**Be Passionate**" about what they want and have a burning desire to reach their goals and the goals of the company.

'E – They are prepared to "**Extend Their Comfort Zone**" and on a daily basis to step outside it. They are not afraid to speak up and share their ideas, be creative and innovate. They are not afraid to make difficult decisions or tackle difficult problems – especially if it involves making sure the customer is happy.

'L – They know that "**Lies and Luck Don't Work**" because they are people of integrity. They do not rely on luck; instead they are proactive in creating opportunities for the company to grow and develop.

'I – They are the kind of people who are able to "**Install Goals**." They understand and believe in the overall purpose of the company. They know their contribution to achieve that goal is essential and they are able to inspire, coach and mentor others to achieve their goals also.

'E – They "**Enjoy Hard Work**", in fact they are the people who work hard and play hard. They are not clock watchers but have the self discipline to tackle the nasty and unsavoury jobs head on and know how to use their time well in order to get things done. They have boundless energy and understand the need to hustle to stay ahead. Remember, good things come to those who wait, but only what is left by those who hustle!

'V – They are "**Very, Very Persistent**" and never give up, especially as they are working to a common goal that they believe in. They refuse to accept no for answer – and why would they if they are working to a common goal that everybody believes in and is passionate about?

'E – They "**Expect Failure**" and are not afraid of risk. They accept that failure is part of the journey of success so they learn from it and use that wisdom to allow them to make sharper judgements and take greater calculated risks in the future.'

Tom waited until Lucy had stopped writing then added a final comment for her to note down.

'Lucy, these kinds of leaders are team players and they totally focus on their customers. They know what is going on in their industry and market place and with their competitors. Their total priority is to focus on growth and innovation and have completely happy long-term customers. Enterprise leaders achieve results, and if Amroze Technology had operated with 2000 employees embracing the enterprise leadership mindset, then I doubt you would be in the situation you are in now.'

Lucy knew he was right, but knowing the answer was only part of the solution. 'Well, I absolutely agree with you, but how do we create a company of enterprise leaders from where we are now?'

'Don't worry; I don't intend to just leave you hanging without helping you resolve the problem!' Lucy could see how energized Tom was in describing this to her. It was truly something that he believed in and was passionate about and undoubtedly had been the inspiration for his own business.

'Well, to start with, there has to be a purpose: something that everybody in the company can believe in. People need goals to aim towards, and what better goal can there be than to focus on the customer?' He broke off and opened his briefcase and took from it his own notebook. 'I read something yesterday that I made a note of for you. It is a quote by Maharishi Patanjali. This wise old man lived a very long time ago, I think around 250 years BC. What he said then has stood the test of time and applies equally today. When you hear it I'm sure you'll agree it holds the key to unlocking the potential within Amroze Technology.' He flicked over the pages until he found what he was looking for. 'Patanjali said this about purpose:

'"*When you are inspired by some great purpose, some extraordinary project, all your thoughts break their bonds, your mind transcends limitations, your consciousness expands in every direction and you find yourself in a great new and wonderful world. Dormant forces, faculties and tal-*

ents become alive and you discover yourself to be a greater person by far than you ever dreamed yourself to be."

'Now, isn't that a powerful statement? I really believe that this is what Amroze Technology needs to do, to find a new purpose that everybody can believe in. Go right back to the beginning and reignite the passion within the company that was there when Charlie first started it. Begin letting people dream and stretch themselves and achieve more than they ever dreamed possible.'

Lucy felt more optimistic than she had in weeks. Tom's sincerity was obvious, and she felt that he really cared that Amroze sorted itself out and moved forward. His enthusiasm was infectious, and as he stretched his hand towards his empty cup, she hurriedly signalled to the waiter to bring them refills so that he didn't need to break the flow of his conversation with her.

'You cannot underestimate the importance of people having the right purpose, and setting goals that will help them towards that. It might help if I give you an example that my mentor Michael used with me. I mentioned it very briefly last week when we were talking about the importance of persistence, but I think in detail it is a great example for understanding the power of goals. Michael Redford reminded me of the very first US space programme as a way of explaining purpose and goals. That programme was inspired by President John F. Kennedy's vision to put a man on the moon and return him safely to earth before the 1960s had ended. At the time, the idea was almost inconceivable, it was the stuff of science fiction, and no one had any idea whether it really could be achieved. It was the president's inspiration to reach that goal in that timeframe, but it was the team who shared that vision and believed in the purpose that made it happen.'

Tom was smiling to himself, and Lucy asked him what he was thinking about as obviously he was remembering something pleasurable and interesting.

'Come on; tell me what is going through your mind?'

'OK, it's a story I wanted to share with you sometime and now seems like the moment. I heard it a long time ago from my mentor Michael and it really sums up for me the power of purpose and having a team that believes in your biggest stretch goals. One day at the start of the space project, President Kennedy was visiting the space centre where the Apollo programme was based and where the rockets were being developed. It was typical of the president that he took time to speak with as many people as he could in the facility and one of those he singled out to talk to was a man sweeping the floor. The president asked this man what his job was at the space centre. The man responded immediately by saying "I'm helping put a man on the moon, Mr President." He knew he was part of a bigger picture and what to some people may be seen as menial work, an insignificant activity, was actually as essential part of the team work that allowed the USA to fulfil its vision.

'Every single person needs to believe, and to play their part. That man demonstrated the sort of passion and belief in a purpose that you need to achieve your goals. Putting a man on the moon is one of man's greatest achievements. It was a massive stretch goal, but because of the power of belief, the power of a team and the sole focus of getting a man on the moon before December 31st, 1969, the impossible was achieved. Now think back to the quote I gave you from Patanjali and tell me whether that man sweeping the floor didn't just perfectly demonstrate exactly what he was saying?'

Lucy thought it was a great example and made a note to include it in her presentation to Stephen. 'Yes, absolutely, and I can really see now that a clear purpose is what Amroze Technology needs. When you described it, I could see that to put a man on the moon the whole team must be strong leaders, or possess the right attitudes and individually be those enterprise leaders that you talked about. But let's get back to Amroze specifically. Our new CEO is due to start in a week's time so just how does he fit into all of this?'

Tom good-humouredly acknowledged her attempt to keep to the focus of her project. 'Good point. Well, as the overall leader, it is his job to set the direction, goals and purpose of the company and inspire and motivate the rest of the team to achieve those "big picture" goals. In other words, it is his job to create belief. It's interesting that you called him the new CEO, as in reality the job title of CEO disguises what he is really there to do. Stephen's new role is primarily to drive change and achieve goals. That is what your company needs more than anything right now: goals and change. It will be Stephen's job to make that happen, but from what you have told me and what I know of him, he sounds the right man for the job.'

Lucy had picked up on Tom's emphasis on goals and change. 'So you are saying that when Stephen sets the goals, he must make sure that everybody buys into them and believes them so that change can happen?'

'Exactly that,' replied Tom. 'If the team does not believe in the goals, vision or purpose, or are not passionately connected with them, then the company has very little chance of achieving them. How could America have landed a man on the moon if everybody working on the space programme did not believe 100% it could be done? If doubt had set in, then the project would have been doomed. As I'm sure you know, passion and enthusiasm are contagious, and so too are doubt and cynicism. We all have two dogs on our shoulders: the one on your left shoulder is positive and says "we can do it"; the other is negative and says "no way – it can never be done". Which one prevails is entirely up to you, because the one that dominates is the one you feed the most. If you keep saying it can be done, it will be done; if you say it can't, then it won't. So communicating positively is an essential part of a leader's role.'

Tom paused as their drinks arrived and then continued to give her the clearest possible explanation.

'Let me put it another way. In any company, its greatest asset is its team of people. Business is all about people. At 5pm when the staff leave for the day, there is no company because without the staff the company doesn't function. If you like, it ceases to exist. Also, without customers – who are also people – really! – there would be no sales, and without people to create products and services there would be nothing to sell to customers. Therefore the quality, morale and motivation of the people are everything. If the people do not believe, just as I explained with the examples of a football team and the man on the moon, how can success come? Belief is everything.

'Now, the question I think you were asking about Stephen is how you create belief within a team or with customers. The answer is communication. You must talk to your team and explain to them what the vision is, what the specific goals are and why you as a leader have decided to do this. This is Stephen's first task when he arrives and it is his most important one. You must explain to customers the benefits of your product or service and to do that you must constantly persuade and influence them towards your point of view, and Stephen has to do the same thing within the company itself. That is all business is really, the power to influence. That is why the big PR and advertising companies are so well paid, because they understand human psychology. They have the ability to influence us to the point where we start to believe one particular product is better for us than another. It is crazy really, but if you stick a branded logo on the same product as an unbranded product, then we will pay more for it, just because we believe in the value of the brand.' Tom stopped, and gave an apologetic smile. 'Sorry, I was getting off track for a moment there. Let's get back to communication. Think about this for a moment. What is the number one reason for divorce?'

Lucy caught herself smiling as she thought, here we go off on another tangent! For some reason, she felt she knew the answer, and after running through possibilities in her head for a moment she realized she had read an article on just that subject recently. 'I know this,' she said as she looked over at Tom. 'It's what you're talking about. It's communication, or rather, the lack of it'. Tom had taken the opportunity to drink some of his coffee while she thought about her reply and as he lowered his cup he gave her a congratulatory nod.

'Spot on and my point is that marriages are no different to business relationships really. It doesn't make any difference whether that relationship is with your employees or your customers. What is important is that all relationships are built on trust and trust must be earned. The biggest breakdown of trust occurs when there is a lack of communication. If you, as a leader, fail to communicate with your team then first of all concern will creep in when problems start to arise. Next thing that happens is that concern will turn to worry and ultimately that becomes doubt – or lack of confidence or belief in the person, product or situation. The way to stop doubt creeping in is to keep feeding the positive dog. It will then be the one who barks the loudest.'

Lucy thought that with a Labrador on each shoulder she'd collapse before feeding either of them but knew what Tom was getting at and understood the power of positive and negative thinking.

'It is therefore the job of the leader to make sure the communication within the teams below and above them is clear, concise, honest and positive. They must make sure that all communication helps reinforce the belief of the team; that it can and will achieve its goals. Now obviously that is not just the responsibility of the new CEO when he joins, it is the responsibility of all enterprise leaders within the company. By that I mean everyone, starting with the receptionist who deals with customers because it is vital he or she believes in the company and can create belief in the customers' eyes, and that belief must go all the way through to the senior management team. Remember President Kennedy and the man who swept the floors? Every single person must feel they are part of the company's goals and then they will all focus on it together. The key here is to make sure everybody in the company is on the same page or "on message" as they say in politics. Give me your notebook for a second, will you?' Lucy was a bit surprised but willingly passed it across the table to him and watched as he drew the top half of a pyramid on one side of the page and then drew the bottom part of a pyramid on the other side of the page. He then lay the book open in front of both of them and flicked the page so she saw both sides.

'From my experience, most companies look like this. Two separate halves. But in my view, the vision and purpose that management has, which is the top half of the pyramid, simply does not align with the vision and purpose of the rest of the company, which is the bottom half of the pyramid. That is a disaster for a company and is the direct result of poor leadership and poor communication. If the goals and purpose are sound enough and well thought through, then it should be possible to get everybody aligned. I want to emphasize to you Lucy that this is something Stephen will have to tackle straight away. It cannot wait. Now, clearly, not everybody will agree with everything all the time; that is why it is vital to have the means to listen to the views of every single person in the company, and why everybody must be prepared to step outside their comfort zone and speak up. You must make it clear to Stephen that it is essential for Amroze Technology to get a common agreement that everybody can believe in and get behind.' He pushed the notebook back across the table to her and Lucy took that as a signal that she could continue with her note taking.

'Communication is a two-way process, Lucy, and management must never forget that. One key reason that management has to listen to everyone is because many of the staff are actually closer, and have more interaction on a regular basis with the customers than management do. Once the purpose has been agreed and communicated, and a plan has been worked out on how to get there, then the whole company must focus on executing that plan. It really is that simple. Where I think Amroze Technology needs to go, is wherever your customers want to go. Never forget, they are the ones who pay the bills, so you had better listen to them!'

Tom leaned back and looked seriously at her. She sensed that he wanted to be certain that she had really understood what he had meant. He picked up his coffee and drank. He waited a moment and then continued.

'Lucy, this has been the final piece of the puzzle for you. Now you know how to reignite the entrepreneurial spirit within Amroze – or indeed any company. You will meet with Stephen next Monday to give him your report and feedback and I hope learning about I BELIEVE, WE BELIEVE and THEY BELIEVE has helped you understand what is going wrong and what needs to be done to fix it. Now it's up to you to write that report in a way that makes it clear what the options are, and makes Stephen see the sense in accepting your recommendations.'

Lucy closed her notebook with a feeling of completeness. 'I really appreciate what you have done, Tom. I feel like I have a blueprint here to regenerate Amroze and I will make sure

Stephen understands how important implementing a new belief system is for the company's survival. Now I see how to write the report, but if I need some fine tuning can I come back to you on Friday?'

'Sure, just give me a ring. But Lucy, I don't think you need any more help. I can see you BELIEVE, and that is all it takes to convince Stephen – that and a great piece of writing!' They both laughed and began to gather up their bags and coats as the waiter brought over their bill.

TOM'S ADVICE

- Great leaders inspire teams to achieve greatness. They fill the team with passion, desire and belief
- Tom's philosophy is about I BELIEVE (the leader), WE BELIEVE (the team) and THEY BELIEVE (the customer)
- It is 'enterprise leaders' who bring the traits and thinking of entrepreneurs to the company. These traits are:

I — 'I Believe' — Enterprise leaders believe in themselves, their products and services and their company. They create belief within the team

B — 'Be Passionate and Want it' — Enterprise leaders are passionate about what they do and instil that passion and desire in others.

E — 'Extend Your Comfort Zone' — Enterprise leaders are comfortable feeling uncomfortable and inspire others to step outside their own personal comfort zone and challenge their fears and limiting beliefs head on

L — 'Lies and Luck Don't Work' — Enterprise leaders are honest with themselves and others and do not rely on luck. They are growth-focused and create opportunity for themselves, the team and their company

I — 'Install Goals' — Enterprise leaders have a clear purpose for what they and the

company want to achieve. They inspire
others to believe passionately in that goal

E — 'Enjoy Hard Work' — Enterprise leaders
and their team work hard and play hard. They
are disciplined and have fun at work (because
they are passionate about what they do)

V — 'Very, Very Persistent' — Enterprise leaders
do not give up or accept no for an answer.
The teams they are part of believe in their
goals and work hard to achieve them

E — 'Expect Failure'. Enterprise leaders recognize
that success and failure go hand in hand
— and that you cannot have success without
failure. They are not afraid of failure and are
prepared to try things that others are not.
They recognize that it is from failure that
wisdom comes and that it is from wisdom and
experience that judgement comes. Only with
judgement can larger calculated risks be taken

- Enterprise leaders know their market,
  their competitors and their industry
- Enterprise leaders understand that a clear
  common purpose and open communication
  is key to uniting a company
- Lack of communication is often the reason for
  a breakdown in relationships. Only communication
  can create belief (i.e. WE BELIEVE)

- The role of the CEO (supported by enterprise leaders) is to drive change and achieve the company's goals. Only by creating unity behind common goals that everybody believes in and understands can this be done
- Talented people are the company's greatest asset; without people, there is no company
- The vision of the management must be aligned with the understanding and purpose of the rest of the company. Without alignment, success will be elusive.

Chapter Nine

After her last meeting with Tom, Lucy had plenty of material and a lot to think about. She spent the rest of the week outlining what she wanted to say by going through her notes again and getting her thoughts straight so she could do justice to all the things she had learned. She began working on the report for Stephen in earnest and was due to hand it to him first thing on the following Monday morning. Lucy was someone who always liked to be well prepared and preferred to be ahead of a deadline, so she was not too put out when she received an unexpected phone call from Stephen on the Thursday afternoon asking if she could email him the report on Saturday morning. He explained that he would like to read it then and see her in person on the Sunday to talk through her findings. Stephen knew that he would have a lot of meetings to attend on Monday with investors, management and staff and he wanted to have Lucy's information ahead of time so he was going well prepared. Lucy agreed she could do that, and as she put the phone down she took a deep breath. She was on schedule for the original target, but this meant stepping up the pace and Stephen's call energized her to meet the new deadline.

Lucy knew that she only had one chance to get this report right; once Stephen had seen it there would be no opportunity to add to it or amend it so it was important that it was clear, concise and had recommendations based on fact not speculation. She mentally settled in, asked the secretary to take her calls, stocked up the coffee machine and then sat at her desk with her notebook and her outline of recommendations so far. She wanted to take her time to think through all that she had learned from her interviews and all that she had learned from Tom. As she looked back over the past three weeks, she realized that she had a much deeper understanding of the problems within the company and also, a much clearer view of what needed to be done to fix them. She could see that the answers were already there in the responses and attitudes of the customers and employees. They had freely expressed their views to her, but in the past few years nobody else had listened to them and that was the main reason that the company was heading in the wrong direction.

Lucy was a woman on a mission. She resolutely ignored all non-essential mail and messages and kept the local sandwich delivery service on speed dial so she didn't miss lunch. She pinned a large note to her wall saying 'SATURDAY IS DEADLINE DAY!' but Friday evening saw her still at her desk. She had actually finished the report earlier that afternoon, but on reading it through she saw areas where she could improve it and had taken Tom up on his offer to check things through with him. She knew how important to the future of Amroze Technology this document might be so she happily put in the extra time and effort and Tom had been very supportive. She smiled as she remembered him saying just before they finished their call that it sounded like she had become the first enterprise leader at Amroze, and he was delighted by her enthusiasm and passion for the task. She had to admit that it had felt good to be so involved and to know she was making a difference. After their call, she worked on into the evening and the building got quieter and quieter as everyone else left for the weekend. Finally, just before midnight she read once more the covering email she had written to Stephen and double checked that the report was attached. Lucy knew she was tired and had to admit that in moments of exhaustion in the past she had sent emails and forgotten the attachment and then had to send another one apologizing for it. This time she made absolutely sure before pressing the send button. As she watched her outbox empty, she felt content that she had given Stephen the best possible report she could. She could now only hope that it gave him the insights he needed before he arrived at the company on Monday.

Going home, she collapsed gratefully into bed and slept right through to 9am on Saturday morning. Knowing that Stephen wanted to see her on Sunday she knew that there was nothing more she could do on the work front and decided to spend the day relaxing to recharge her batteries ready for the meeting with him the following day. She had invited a couple of friends for supper and as she relaxed with a glass of wine she basked in the sense of achievement that comes with the end of a project.

Dinner with friends had been the perfect way to forget any anxieties she might have felt about seeing Stephen, so after another good night's sleep she arrived at his house at 11am on Sunday morning in a positive and confident mood. She had never been to his present home and the large detached house was set on a private estate which made her reflect that Stephen had certainly been highly successful since the days when they had studied their MBAs together. Then he had lived in a modest flat near the city centre, and could never find a place to park on the crowded street outside. His wife, Trinity, answered the door and she showed Lucy through to a study at the back of the house. It was large and elegantly furnished with an old oak desk and a big comfortable sofa that looked from the indentations in it as if Stephen often lay back there to read. The room overlooked a garden with a lawn, trees and the glint of water where there was an ornamental pond. Lucy had wandered over to the large picture window to look at the view and so she nearly missed Stephen's greeting as he came into the room. Looking relaxed in his own environment, he came forward to shake her hand.

'Lucy, it's really good to see you again. If you have the time after our meeting we'd love you to stay for lunch and we can have a chat about what's going on in your life. She smiled back, 'Lunch would be great,' and sat on the sofa that he indicated to her.

'Now can I offer you a drink of something before we start?'

'No, nothing for me, thanks. As you will have seen from the report, Amroze certainly needs some focused attention.' He noticed she was eager to get on and reminded himself that this had been a huge undertaking for her. He sat down with her on the sofa and put the report on the oak coffee table in front of them.

'I was right that you were the best person for this particular project, Lucy. When I'd heard you had been fast-tracked at Amroze I really wanted to have you working on this because I knew you would have a lot of input to offer. I really pushed the chairman to give me your exclusive time to get this job done. I remember how dogged you were when you made your mind up to achieve something, so I knew you wouldn't let me down. Truly, I am really grateful you took it on. I needed to have this done by someone I could trust to be honest, and who I knew could handle getting right down to the bones of the company and finding out what the problems were.

'First of all, let me say that the report is excellent and has given me a lot to think about. It has certainly made for interesting reading and the way you have laid it out has made it easy to see the logical progression of how the situation at Amroze has deteriorated.'

Although she knew she had done a good job, Lucy was grateful to get praise for it and to know he appreciated the work that had gone into it. 'I'm pleased to hear it and it was good for me too. I actually really enjoyed preparing it and meeting all the staff and customers to get their views. I'm just sorry the outlook is not better.' She glanced at his face as she spoke and was reassured to see that he didn't look as worried about it as she had thought he might.

'I think the outlook could be very positive. Yes, there are certainly problems and you have done a great job in outlining what they are, but as you rightly point out in your report, the one thing that is needed is change and coming in as a new CEO that is easier for me to implement than for someone already in there. I am well aware that this is an opportunity that we need to grasp and we can only do that by recognizing that the only way to turn around our fortunes is to embrace change. Fundamentally that is what my job is all about and I am sure that's why Amroze Technology wanted me because they know that is how I operate.' He indicated the report on the table. 'Look, Lucy, the reason I wanted you to come over today is so that I could hear directly from you in your own words what you have found in the past few weeks. Your report is excellent, as I said, but I want to hear it from you in person.

I want you to give me a real sense of how you feel about what you found. I really liked the way you structured your report around Tom's I BELIEVE, WE BELIEVE and THEY BELIEVE. It is a great foundation that I intend to build on – leadership, teams and customers. Those are the things that are really at the heart of any company and you have made me think about this in a new and interesting way. So, let's hear it, just tell me exactly what you think about the situation at Amroze and don't worry, I can take it!'

He smiled encouragingly at her so Lucy took a deep breath and gathered her thoughts. She then began to walk Stephen through her findings using examples and quotes from the commercial world just as Tom had done. She explained in detail the themes of customer belief, product innovation and staff morale. She impressed on him the need for belief, passion and purpose; installing goals that every employee can get behind. He listened intently, nodding and jotting things down as she spoke.

'Stephen, just imagine what we could achieve if we really were able to ignite that talent and give people a clear purpose and vision to work towards. I know the ideas on how to turn this company around are within us and to be honest, at this point, the only real resource we have is ideas. Simon Ross, the chief financial officer, made it very clear to me that we cannot afford to spend on new staff and that he is going to recommend to you that we cut our workforce and Gracie Smith, your HR director, said the same thing to me. Now, if we do have to do that, we could consider adopting Jack Welsh's formula at General Electric and lose the bottom 10%, which are those who are underperforming. Obviously we would need to do some analysis to ascertain if it would work in this environment but let's do everything we can to keep the best talent within the company. Just imagine what we could do with a motivated, passionate team. We would be unstoppable – just like we were when Charlie was there. I know you never met him, but everyone who worked with Charlie that I spoke with all said the same things: he was passionate about his work, the company, the employees and most of all the customers, and he communicated that to everyone he came into contact with.'

Stephen acknowledged her point. He had never met Charlie, but the man was certainly a legend in the industry and his reputation still stood very high. The regard people held him in had definitely been a factor in Amroze's success and Stephen wanted to get back that kind of pride and respect both internally and in the industry generally. Lucy again paused as she could see he was thinking, but he indicated with his hand that she should carry on.

'I know we are going to need some big ideas to turn this around, but we must not be afraid to try them and even be prepared to fail if necessary. Not every idea will work, but we must go for the ones we all believe in. If we do fail, we should fail fast, learn and move on, but we should not be afraid of taking a risk. We should not let fear of failure stop us. I think in many ways that has been the problem that has crept up on us in recent years. Since Amroze Technology went public there has been a definite shift in attitude, much more conservative and less willing to go out on a limb. We have become too risk averse and complacent. In the early days, we tried so many different ideas and some worked, some didn't – but we weren't afraid to try them. We let our customers be the final decision-maker on what worked, but we tried, we innovated, we led the industry and we made our customers believe in us. Where did that spirit go?

'At this point, I believe this is what we need to do again. We need to set big goals, massive goals, we need to find our own "man on the moon" type of project. We can do it. I read an article recently by Howard Schultz, the founder of Starbucks, which I really think sums it up well. He said:

"People want to be part of something larger than themselves. They want to be part of something they're really proud of, that they'll fight for, that they trust."

'I believe he is absolutely right. We need to give our staff that. We need to inspire them to achieve the impossible. If that is putting a man in space or having another thousand happy new customers within 12 months, then that is what we must do. But for that to happen, some things must change, and change must become a word we are comfortable with. We need to start being comfortable being uncomfortable! I know that change can seem a threatening word to many people, but it lies at the heart of what we have to do. Don't just take my word for it!' She gave Stephen a quick glance.

'Let me quote Darwin. He said:

"It is not the strongest of the species that survive, nor the most intelligent, but the one most responsive to change."

'Now that has got to be us. We have spent too much time standing still and now we must change, become agile, fast and open to new ideas. It is the only way forward and it is also the way our customers and new customers want us to go. To find the right way forward we will need to have a clear purpose that the whole company can passionately believe in. Then we will be able to keep and attract excellent people, the best and brightest in the industry, and that is the way we will be able to turn Amroze Technology around. Stephen, you need to shake things up a bit!'

'Lucy, I could not agree with you more. I told you that the main reason I asked you to come here today was because although I read your report I really wanted to hear you talk and get a sense of how you felt about Amroze Technology. What I heard very clearly from what you said is that you still believe and your enthusiasm is really infectious. If I didn't believe before, I would certainly believe after listening to you. You can trust me when I tell you that this confidence is what I want in the company and that is what the company really needs. You even say it in your report and I agree that we need leaders at all levels who share your passion, belief and drive and are not afraid to speak up or even fail.'

Lucy felt a great sense of relief. She had known Stephen would listen to her and give her his full attention, but she hadn't been sure he would so wholeheartedly agree with her conclusions. She sat back against the cushions and experienced a great rush of energy when she realized that Stephen meant what he said and that change was definitely going to happen. Stephen leaned forward and tapped the report on the coffee table.

'You did a terrific job on this and after hearing you speak, I am confident you are one of the people who will help me drive the company forward. I can tell you now, that doing this project was important for me, but it was also important for you. I wanted to see what you made of it. It was, if you like, an "apprenticeship" to see how you coped with a large and difficult project that took you into the company at all levels. I have been monitoring your progress, and the feedback I have had from Tom was all positive. He didn't breach your confidentiality, but he did tell me that you were someone I should promote and use to make the company great again.'

Lucy hadn't been sure where this speech was going, and she was a little unnerved when she heard she had been 'on trial'. 'Good job I didn't know about it!' was her immediate thought but the rest of what he was saying definitely made her sit up and take notice.

'I want to make you an offer, a job offer. I want our company to share the values you have outlined, and I want our staff to love this company as if it was their own. I want them to think "What would I do if it was my company?" or even "What would the founder do?" when they are confronted with difficult decisions. I want them to understand our clear purpose and buy into it and passionately believe it. I want them to appreciate our customers and always put them first because they are the ones who have the cash. We need that cash because that is the lifeblood of any company – and at the moment, that is the one thing which is in short supply in Amroze.

'If we are to change we need leaders at all levels. We need people who live and breathe your messages of I, WE and THEY BELIEVE and I want you to help me make that happen. When I read your report, it was clear to me that I needed to have somebody in the company I could rely on to help me implement that. That is why I would like you to agree to be our new "Chief Enterprise Leader". It is a new post, created just for you and it will be your job to fill Amroze Technology with other enterprise leaders who share the same mindset as you. I want you to motivate everyone to be driven to grow this company by embracing innovation, change and focusing on our customers. What do you think? Does it sound like something you want to do?'

'Chief Enterprise Leader. Does it sound like something I want to do?!' thought Lucy. It certainly sounded good, and it was being created just for her. Lucy was surprised and delighted, not least because after three weeks of hearing from unhappy customers and disillusioned staff, this was the last thing she had expected to be offered. It was an incredible compliment and it was something she could not say no to. A promotion to a position where she could put Tom's BELIEVE philosophy truly to the test was irresistible and it took only a few seconds for her to say yes.

Stephen offered her his hand. 'Let's shake on it. I am delighted you agreed, but then I never doubted you would, just like I had every confidence you were the right person to undertake this project for me. And you proved me 100% right – just keep doing that and we will stay good friends!' She laughed with him and reached across to return his handshake and seal their agreement.

After lunch, Lucy left Stephen's house almost walking on air. She was so excited and enthused about the challenge ahead, she could hardly wait to start putting it into practice. She was totally confident that if she was true to the principles of I, WE and THEY BELIEVE it would be the key to reigniting the entrepreneurial spirit that made Amroze Technology great in the first place. She got into her car and drove a short way from Stephen's house and then pulled over and got out her mobile phone to call Tom and tell him the good news.

Chapter Ten

EPILOGUE – 100 DAYS ON

It had been a long haul, but everyone had got involved. Stephen had been true to his word and made change his priority. One of the first things he had done was to give everyone in the company a business-style card with Amroze's logo and five bullet points on it. He had asked everyone to carry this with them at all times or display it prominently where they worked. He had based the points on the views expressed in Lucy's interviews and had consulted with many representatives of each department so that everyone had put some input into the finished card. Lucy had hers in her wallet and she took it out frequently to remind herself of what the new priorities were.

Amroze Technology:
- I BELIEVE, WE BELIEVE, THEY BELIEVE
- Always put the customers first
- Watch the Cash!
- Constant and never-ending innovation
- It's your company – what do you do next?

She tucked the card back into her purse as she hurried across to the lifts to take her straight up to the large boardroom and hospitality suite on the top floor. Today was a big day, because Stephen had organized a '100 day' celebration for the Amroze staff worldwide. Obviously, because everyone knew that cash was still tight, it was not going to be lavish, or an expensive celebration but staff at all the offices around the world had devised their own celebration. What they all had in common was that they were all going to see a specially prepared video message from Stephen as part of the celebration. Lucy had been involved in the planning, and it had been arranged that the timing of the video would follow the sun around the world as it touched all the regional offices and staff. They all were celebrating in their different ways and Lucy had helped to coordinate it with all the worldwide offices. She knew that in Japan they had arranged to see the video at the office and then have a breakfast picnic in a nearby park together. In the various US regional offices they had arranged a shared box lunch and a softball game between employees and management with several of the company's first aid volunteers agreeing to stand by in case anyone got over-enthusiastic! The one she would have loved to have attended was in Australia where they were having a beach barbeque in the late afternoon.

At head office they had gone for a 'bring a dish to share' lunch with a party afterwards, to which all employees were invited. Lucy had checked every detail, and now it was time to celebrate. The board room and hospitality suite were filled to overflowing but nobody seemed to mind the crush and Lucy looked around at all the expectant and cheerful faces and marvelled at the change that had taken place in just a few short months. She was standing at the back of the room as Stephen stood up to make his speech. Although it had already been recorded to send to the other Amroze Technology offices, he wanted to make it live and in person for the head office staff. In the short time he had been with the company he could address many individuals by name and give them a personal remark. It had been part of his success, and Lucy felt proud to have been a part of that. Once this was over, she could relax and enjoy the party, and she prepared to listen as Stephen stepped forward to the microphone on the podium. He received a genuine round of applause, which he acknowledged with a smile, and then he waited for everyone to settle down before he began speaking with quiet emphasis on his key points.

'100 days ago we were a company running out of cash, today we have stopped it endlessly flowing outwards and have now got our cash under control. 100 days ago our customers were leaving us, today we have turned that around and we have convinced customers new and old that we are the right choice for them.

'100 days ago our share price was at an all-time low, today we have seen a steady increase in our valuation and only yesterday I received a report from an industry analyst that recommended us as a buy and a growth stock.'

Here he was interrupted with cheers and more applause, which he acknowledged with a smile.

'Yes, I thought that would please everyone and especially those of you with large stock holdings!' People laughed and Lucy took a quick glance round, noticing that everyone was paying real attention and there was a feeling of camaraderie and team spirit in the room.

'100 days ago we had products that were outdated and did not meet the needs of our customers. Now, I appreciate that it has not been possible to fix that in this short time, but we have listened to our customers and we have a clear road map to develop our products and our customers are ready to start believing in us again.

'100 days ago most of our employees had doubts about the future of the company, and their own future within it. Today as I look around at us here, I can see a huge difference because now you too believe in Amroze Technology and its future growth, as I most certainly do.

'We have made tremendous progress over the past three months, and of course that does not come without some measures that have been tough, but necessary. I profoundly regret that we have had to lose some of the team along the way to bring our cash under control, but those of you who remain are, I believe, the real talent within the company and you deserve to have Amroze investing time and money in you. Of course at the moment, that is more time than money!' People laughed and Lucy could see that they trusted him, and believed in what he was doing. That is what had made the difference. As the laughter died down, Stephen continued.

'I am doing that because it has been your ideas, creative thinking, passion and belief that has helped us turn the company around. The company is you; without you Amroze Technology is nothing. It is your continued commitment, drive, innovative thinking and focus on our customers that made this company great in the first place. It is those same attributes that will make this company a true market leader again. I want to take this opportunity to personally thank you all for your commitment in turning our company around.' Again he was interrupted by applause, and he returned the gesture by clapping his own hands together and directing it to everyone in the room.

'Thank you and before we all get carried away, let me remind you that our work has only just begun. We have taken the first step and now we must continue to walk forward over what is still going to be rough ground for a while yet. What is different now is that we know where we are going, we believe we will get there and we know why we are going there. This is a different company from the one it was 100 days ago; now it is one of passion, belief and drive. It is one that values its customers and works together as a team. There is no reason we cannot continue for the next 100 days as we did in the first, and again for another 100 days and forward into the future. We will make this company great again and it is you, and your entrepreneurial spirit that will do it. You know what our priorities are – and if you forget then just take out that card I sent all of you and read those five points until you do know! Those priorities reflect the fact that now we have a clear purpose that each one of you – as the enterprise leaders you have become – is contributing to every day in every part of your work here. Now, that's quite enough from me. Enjoy your celebration, you have earned it.'

He stepped down to applause that was wholeheartedly enthusiastic and genuine and several people came forward to shake his hand and congratulate him. Lucy was soon being congratulated herself by many of the staff members she had interviewed. She was really boosted by everyone's positive response to the 100 day celebration and Stephen sought her out later on to add his personal congratulations and once again to say 'well done'. He was looking a little more relaxed, but when he spoke to her he sounded quite serious.

'Lucy, I want to say a special thank you to you for organizing all this. It is thanks to you that over the past 100 days we have achieved an extraordinary amount. Perhaps we have not quite landed a man on the moon yet, but at least we are all clear on our purpose of going to the moon together. What you have done to reinstall the belief back in our company has been exceptional and ultimately your programme to create enterprise leaders at all levels has been the catalyst for our change. Without that change in mindset, we would never have been able to turn the company around. Oh, and though it's small, there is definitely a bonus on its way to you and believe me there will be another one as soon as we can afford it.' Lucy smiled her thanks as his attention was claimed by J.P. Wiseman and from J.P.'s relaxed smile it looked like things were improving on the product side as well. Something else to celebrate for Amroze, and Lucy thought she might have something to celebrate herself soon. Not that she would take up the offer, but in a quieter moment she wanted to tell Stephen about the text she had received that morning from Charlie Gardham. He too had offered his congratulations, but it was the last line of the message that had made her smile. It just said, 'want to come and upgrade my new company?' and that, she knew, was the greatest accolade of all.

WANT TO GO FURTHER?

Having read how enterprise leadership can make a dramatic difference to the performance and success of a company, you can now develop enterprise leaders deep within your organization by visiting www.enterpriseleaders.com.

Brought to you by Enterprise Leaders Worldwide, our leadership development programme unleashes the talent within your organization to develop your very own enterprise leadership style.

Delivered either online, offline or via workshops, Enterprise Leaders Worldwide develops commercially-minded leaders who consistently achieve results against all odds.

www.enterpriseleaders.com

Index

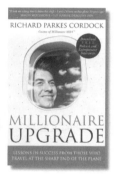

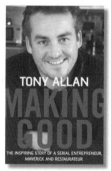
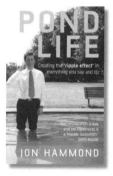